COS**girl!**

PARTIES

how to throw the
best bash ever!

PARTIES

how to throw the best bash ever!

by lauren a. greene

HEARST BOOKS
A division of Sterling Publishing Co., Inc.

New York / London
www.sterlingpublishing.com

Designed by Georgia Rucker Design

Library of Congress Cataloging-in-Publication Data
Greene, Lauren A.
  CosmoGIRL! parties: how to throw the best bash ever / by Lauren Greene.
  p. cm.
Includes index.
ISBN-13: 978-1-58816-679-1
1. Parties. 2. Entertaining. I. Cosmo girl. II. Title.   III. Title: Cosmo girl parties.
GV1471.G773 2008
793.2--dc22
                           2007045377

10 9 8 7 6 5 4 3 2 1

Published by Hearst Books
A Division of Sterling Publishing Co., Inc.
387 Park Avenue South, New York, NY 10016

CosmoGIRL! and Hearst Books are trademarks of Hearst Communications, Inc.

www.cosmogirl.com

For information about custom editions, special sales, premium and corporate purchases, please contact Sterling Special Sales Department at 800-805-5489 or specialsales@sterlingpublishing.com.

Distributed in Canada by Sterling Publishing
℅ Canadian Manda Group, 165 Dufferin Street
Toronto, Ontario, Canada M6K 3H6

Distributed in Australia by Capricorn Link (Australia) Pty. Ltd.
P.O. Box 704, Windsor, NSW 2756 Australia

Manufactured in China

Sterling ISBN 978-1-58816-679-1

contents

susan's note

Hey CosmoGIRL!s,

Do you **love** parties? Who doesn't, really? But there are those of us who know how to throw 'em, and those of us who know how to be great guests. I'm the latter. As a guest, I will circulate and talk to **everyone**, make people feel welcome, sample all the food, and all-in-all have a super time—but what I'm *not* so good at is the planning part. Why? I'm not sure. Maybe it's because I see all the fabulous parties people throw and I get intimidated… I think, how could mine ever be that **cool**? But here's the thing: I have a feeling that some of you out there feel the same way I do, right? And that's why we've been creating entertaining stories in *CosmoGIRL!* for years. So that even if you don't have an inner party-planner lurking inside you, you can fake it with the best of them! From **unique** birthdays to **festive** holiday gatherings and every occasion in between, we've got fresh ideas for invitations, food, drinks, decorations, and play lists—all the details you need to throw an unforgettable, one-of-a-kind get-together.

With this book as your guide, you'll throw a party that people are **impressed with** because you thought of **everything** right down to the strawberry garnish on every glass or the spill of confetti on the tabletops. And here's the **best** part: you won't have to think of everything, because we've done it for you. You just need to get **inspired**, follow along with our easy how-to's, and soon everyone will be asking you, "So when's your next **fab** soiree?!"

E-mail me at **susan@cosmogirl.com** with your party questions and ideas. Look for them in a future issue of the magazine! And in the meantime, **party on**, CosmoGIRL!s!

Love,

how to use this book:

Party planning is a hands-on activity, which can sometimes leave your hands full. This book will not only inspire amazing themes, it will also keep you organized. Think of it as a guide, scrapbook, and planner all in one. Use the handy lists, calendars, and note pages to jot down tasks, keep track of your RSVPs, and even store receipts or clippings of party ideas you rip out from magazines. And throughout the book don't forget to look for a few added extras—check out the key below. Now turn the page and let's get this party started!

KEY

Spend a lot or spend a little—look for the dollar signs to find parties in your price range

$ on the cheap

$$ middle of the road

$$$ blow-out bash

ö CG! Ouch: Party Edition
This symbol will lead you to humiliating party tales that will make your hair curl!

! Party Lines: Look for this symbol to get hot tips and advice from fellow *CosmoGirl!* readers.

CHAPTER 1

party **planning**

party **planning**

There's nothing more exciting than the anticipation of a big party, especially when you're the one putting it all together. But way before your guests arrive and you're the center of their attention, you've got to focus *your* attention on the details. From choosing a theme and setting a

budget to shopping for supplies and finding the right favor, there's lots to do. It may even feel overwhelming at times— but don't sweat it! We've got checklists, timelines, and charts to guide you through the whole process so your party will come together faster than your friends can RSVP! Ready? Get Set. Prep!

the **countdown**

No matter what kind of party you're planning, it generally takes 4 to 6 weeks of preparation. Staying organized is the key to success. Use this timeline to help you count-down to the big day. Fill in important dates in the Calendar (page 12) as you go so you can keep on track!

four to six weeks before

- Pick the date.
- Create the guest list.
- Send a "save the date" e-mail if it's a holiday party, graduation party, or during another busy party season.
- Set the budget (see page 20 for more help).
- If you plan to splurge on a special service like renting a karaoke machine or hiring a makeup artist to do nails, price out and reserve them as far ahead of time as you can.

three to four weeks before

- Choose the theme.
- Make a list of decorations.
- Think about the kind of invite and favors you want.
- Gather supplies you already have around the house, then make a shopping list of the remaining items you need.

two to three weeks before

- Make or buy invites and mail or hand out.
- Shop for favors (if you plan to order them, allow extra time for shipping).
- Buy remaining party décor.

one week before

- Put together gift bags or favors if they need organizing. Store in a safe place.
- Plan out the room—figure out how you'll arrange seating, where you'll hang decorations, where you'll serve the food, etc.
- Confirm the guest list. Check with any guests who haven't RSVP'd.
- Make any food or desserts you can freeze ahead of time.

PARTY TIME!

two days before

◻ Shop for groceries—ask a parent or sibling to come along to help.

the day before

◻ Buy flowers.

◻ Clean the party area, arrange furniture, and set up decorations (ask your family nicely to stay out of the room once it's prepared).

◻ Set the table.

◻ Create any centerpieces.

◻ Make hors d'oeuvres. Store in fridge.

the morning of

◻ Pick up any special decorations or items you may have ordered (i.e., helium balloons, a custom cake, etc.).

◻ Straighten up the bathroom, the entryway, and any other areas guests might be in.

four hours before

◻ Prepare food and/or drinks (except for fizzy drinks).

◻ Check party room. Make any last minute changes or fixes.

◻ Start to get ready yourself.

one hour before

◻ Arrange hors d'oeuvres, chips, and snacks on your coffee table.

◻ Be sure any embarrassing personal items like naked baby pictures, tubes of zit cream, or your bedtime bite guard are hidden away!

twenty minutes to go!

◻ Mix fizzy drinks.

◻ Start music.

◻ Light candles.

◻ Pour drinks so they are ready to hand out as guests arrive.

◻ Relax and look gorgeous!!!!

CG! tip: Cut your work in half and turn decorating the house and whipping up drinks into a pre-party get-together. Invite a few close friends over the night before (or the afternoon of) to help set the mood—your guests will have as much fun in the scene as they do creating it!

calendar

sun	mon	tues	wed	thurs	fri	sat

month:

sun	mon	tues	wed	thurs	fri	sat

party **planning**

v.i.p. list
very important partiers

Now that you've decided to plan a party, it's time to make the guest list and send out the invites!

four rules of guest lists

1. Mix it up. Like the cast of an addictively good reality show, a great party needs variety to spice things up! Shake up your usual group of characters with some interesting fresh blood. Why not ask that cute new foreign exchange student or the artsy girl you met at your after-school job?

2. Size matters. Keep in mind the size of your party space. Rubbing shoulders with guests can be sexy, but if you're smooshed together like sardines, it can get uncomfortable and sweaty—and that's *not* hot! If you're partying outdoors, feel free to super-size the guest list, but if your soiree is going to be confined to a small area you'll want to reel it in.

3. More is less. Although everyone loves you (of course!), not everyone will be able to attend—for whatever reason. To make up for the "Nos" you'll get, plan to invite the number of guests you'd actually like to be at your party, plus an extra five.

> **CG! tip:** Create a party database on your computer with all your friends' e-mails, addresses, and phone numbers. Update the list as needed. Then each time you throw a party, you'll have all the invite info you need right at your fingertips.

4. Edit guilt-free. Back in your elementary school days, when mom and dad footed the whole bill, you may have had the luxury of inviting your entire class. But if you're financing the festivities now, you might have to pick and choose. Deciding whom to invite is tough but partying is supposed to be enjoyable, not a stressful, pressure-packed chore. So include as many guests as your budget allows but be careful not to leave out anyone who would expect an invite. You can always invite guests that were left off the list to a future (less expensive) party.

invite 411

Whether you send a casual Evite or hand out something creative or formal, every invitation should include these basics.

didja know?

RSVP stands for *Repondez, S'il Vous Plait,* which is French for "Reply, Please." How *chic!*

Who: The host of the party (that would be you!)

What: The reason for the party (let them know if there's a theme and what the celebration is for)

When: The date (include the day of the week) and the time it starts and ends

Where: The location (even if it's just at your house, make sure to include your full address)

Attire: How to dress and if there's anything special guests need to bring (like a bathing suit)

RSVP: A date to respond by and how to let you know (by phone, text or e-mail)

guest **list**

| Party Theme | | Date | |

Name	
Address	
Cell	Yes
E-mail	No

Name	
Address	
Cell	Yes
E-mail	No

Name	
Address	
Cell	Yes
E-mail	No

Name	
Address	
Cell	Yes
E-mail	No

Use this page to make your guest list and keep track of who's coming. If you're a superpartier, you may want to make copies of the page before you write on it so you'll have extras on hand for all your future festivities!

Party Theme _____ Date _____

Name _____
Address _____
Cell _____ Yes ____
E-mail _____ No ____

Name _____
Address _____
Cell _____ Yes ____
E-mail _____ No ____

Name _____
Address _____
Cell _____ Yes ____
E-mail _____ No ____

Name _____
Address _____
Cell _____ Yes ____
E-mail _____ No ____

party planning

money, money, **money!**

It's time to talk about your (groan!) budget. We know thinking about cash flow is like hanging a big, dark cloud over the sunny fun of planning a party, but spending (and saving) smartly is a crucial part of any well-organized event. And the more you plan, the more you can pay for— cha-ching! Read on for creative ways to manage your money.

five ways to save cash...

1. **Team up.** Plan and host a party with a friend (or maybe two?) and it will be double the fun and half the money. By dividing up all the expenses and pooling your resources, you'll get twice as much party bang for your buck.

2. **Buy in bulk.** Hit the local Costco and save on party-size bags of chips and candy, cases of bottled water or soda, and paper goods. You can also look for cool (and cheap!) favors like discount CDs and books or cute hair accessories.

3. **Build a party arsenal.** At the end of your party, save any usable leftover items like rolls of crepe paper, extra napkins, and swizzle sticks and store them away. Next time you're hosting, you'll have some resources ready to go. Keep adding to the party pot—the more supplies you save, the less money you'll have to spend. Bonus: Your stash will come in handy those times you want to throw an impromptu bash.

4. **Think outside the box.** Be creative and you can make amazing and memorable décor on the cheap: Cut a few branches off a tree, spray them with glitter, hang jeweled necklaces on them, and place them in a vase. Or string a clothesline across the room, blow up photos of your friends on a copier, and pin them up with clothespins.

5. **Save your change.** You'd be surprised how quickly dimes and nickels can add up. Buy a party piggy bank and every time you break a dollar and get back change, pop those coins right in. Keep feeding the pig and soon enough you'll be feeding your friends at your next bash!

Did you know...
that 64 percent of you would rather party at home than schlep to a club? Way to save money and keep it real, *chicas*!

...and four ways to make some!

1. **Set up a parental 401K.** Talk to (don't beg or whine!) your parents and see if you can strike up a deal—if you agree to save or earn X amount of money, they'll match you dollar for dollar.

2. **Make friends with ebay.** Clean out your closet and sell off your junk online. (Come on, you know you don't need those 100 Beanie Babies anymore!)

3. **Earn interest.** Open a "party fund" bank account (get a parent to cosign if you're under 18) and earn interest (free money!) off your savings. Vow to make weekly deposits and use a calendar to remind and motivate you.

4. **Be queen of the odd jobs.** Put the word out to friends, relatives, and neighbors that you're looking to cash in. Try walking dogs, feeding cats, watering plants, raking leaves, babysitting, or washing cars.

cheap, cheap!

Party and specialty stores can be pricey. Try these other ways to stock up and save.

- Dollar stores
- Thrift or vintage stores
- Craft stores
- Drugstores
- Drama department: See if you can arrange to borrow props from your high school.
- Your basement, attic, or garage: You never know what party-perfect supplies you might find.
- Wal-Mart, Kmart, Target, and other discount chains.
- And don't forget to check out the resources on page 132 for more shopping ideas!

party planning

19

budget **breakdown**

	item	price	quantity	✓
invite	cardstock	$		
	markers			
	other (candy, small gifts, etc.)			
décor	balloons			
	flowers			
	fabric			
	candles			
food	hors d'oeuvres			
	chips, nuts			
	entrée			
	desserts			

Fill in all your party necessities along with their prices and total it up. Over budget? Go back and see where you can cut, save, or borrow items to lower costs. Recalculate until you've reached your goal. Then check things off as you purchase them.

	item	price	quantity	✓
drinks	soda	$		
	tea			
	juice			
	garnishes			
tableware	plates			
	cups			
	napkins			
	utensils			
	serving plates & bowls			
favors	fill in supplies to make your favors			
	TOTAL	$		

to-do **list**

Use this page to make your shopping list, or to write down important party related tasks you don't want to forget. Then check them off as you complete each one.

to do ✓

CHAPTER 2

hostess with
the **mostess**

hostess with
the **mostess**

Think of your party as a three-ring circus and you as the ring master, the clown, the tight rope walker, and the beautiful lady on the elephant all rolled into one. That's because it's your job as hostess to take charge, help people have fun, and sidestep any tricky dilemmas—all while looking gorgeous and stress-free. But have no fear, this chapter is loaded with expert advice on party etiquette, ice breaking tricks, party-pooper problem solving, and style suggestions that'll help you fly through your party with the greatest of ease!

party
etiquette 101

You could take an entire class on etiquette, there's so much to learn. But who has time to waste when there are parties to plan?! That's why we put together this crash course. Read up and you'll soon be Miss Behaving!

ground rules

There are some basics when it comes to being a first-rate hostess.

■ **Be on time.** Make sure you plan ahead and give yourself enough time to get everything ready. You don't want guests arriving to a half-dressed hostess! So plan to be dressed and set to go at least 30 minutes before everyone's scheduled to arrive.

■ **Keep an eye on your guests.** If some-one seems shy or uncomfortable, discreetly help her out. Introduce her to a more outgoing friend or give her a fun task that will engage her with other guests—like taking requests for songs.

■ **Circulate through the party.** Try not to let one friend hog your time for too long. *All* of your guests came to see you, so make sure you spread the love, sister!

■ **Flash those pearly whites.** A great smile and a happy attitude are key to hostess success. If you're having a fantastic time, you'll send positive vibes out and it will be hard for others not to join in. So even if you're nervous, stressed, or worried that you will run out of chips, don't let others see you sweat—fake that smile until you make it real!

■ **Say goodnight gracefully.** When it's time to call it a night, give guests the hint by turning down (or turning off) the music and turning on the lights. If that doesn't work, begin gathering and handing out party favors. And always walk your guests to the door and thank them for coming.

mingle all the way

Small talk and mingling can seem scary, especially when you're with people you may not know that well. These easy tips will walk you through it.

■ **Make eye contact.** Stay focused on the person in front of you. Wouldn't you hate to be talking to someone who kept looking around the room or zoning out? Of course! So give your guests the same respect.

■ **Ask questions.** Talking about themselves puts people at ease because they know the topic so well! If you ask a guest about herself, she'll be more likely to feel comfortable with you and will want to continue to chat. Hint: Listen carefully—her answers will spark more conversation.

■ **Act confident and fabulous.** Because, hey, you are! Think about all the amazing things you do (clubs you're in, hobbies you have, etc.), so when it's your turn you'll have plenty to contribute. Still not sure? Before a big party read a cool book, watch an interesting program, or see a new movie to expand your small talk arsenal.

■ **Have an exit strategy.** When it's time to move on, something honest and simple always works, "It's been great talking to you, but would you please excuse me for a while?" Or try a little humor, "I've been eyeing those *(insert yummy hors d'oeuvres name here)* all night and there are only a few left. Do you mind if I make a run for them?"

be my guest

Follow these Do's and Don'ts for being the ideal guest—and if there were an academy award for parties you'd be voted Best Guest!

DO RSVP by the date on the invite.

DO ask the hostess if you can help with anything when you arrive (or ask beforehand if you can bring anything).

DO try to meet at least one new person.

DO treat your friend's home like your own.

DO offer to stay a little later and help clean up.

DO have fun and thank your hostess the next day with a call or e-mail.

DON'T show up with extra or uninvited guests unless you have okayed it with the hostess.

DON'T arrive later than 15-20 minutes past the scheduled time.

DON'T monopolize the hostess—there are other guests who'd like to see her.

DON'T complain to the hostess or criticize the party. (When you throw a party, you can do things your way.)

DON'T wander into other parts of the house alone or go through the hostess's drawers and closets.

DON'T overstay your welcome. If you're the last one left and your hostess is yawning—take the hint and head home.

hostess with the **mostess**

25

get the party
started!

Nothing kills a party quicker than a cloud of awkward silence. If you can hear a pin drop in the room, try one of these party tricks pronto!

would you rather...

Want to get guests talking? Give them one of these choices to ponder and watch the social sparks start to fly!

Would you rather:

. . . always wear wet socks or always wear wet underwear?

. . . spit on everyone you talk to or be spit on by everyone who talks to you?

. . . never be able to laugh or never be able to cry?

. . . talk like Yoda or breathe like Darth Vader for the rest of your life?

. . . have a second head on your body or no head at all?

. . . be naked in front of a group of strangers or a group of friends?

. . . eat only cafeteria food or only airplane food for a year?

laugh factory

Tell a joke...break the ice.

Q: Why did the cookie go to the doctor?

A: It was feeling crummy!

A police officer pulls a man over for speeding and asks him to get out of the car. After looking the man over, he says, "Sir, I couldn't help but notice your eyes are very bloodshot. Have you been drinking?" The man gets indignant and says, "Officer, I couldn't help but notice your eyes are all glazed. Have you been eating doughnuts?"

A pretty girl walks up to the counter at a fabric store and says, "I would like to buy this material for a new dress. How much does it cost?" "Only one kiss per yard," replies the male clerk with a smirk. "That's fine," says the girl. "I'll take ten yards." With excitement and anticipation written all over his face, the clerk quickly measures out the cloth, wraps it up, then teasingly holds it out. The girl snaps up the package, points to the old geezer standing beside her, smiles, and says, "Grandpa will pay the bill!"

Q: Where do cows go to have fun?

A: To the moovies!

lap stack

Play this game and your guests will be cozying up to one another in no time!

Select one person to be the Quiz Master (as hostess you should volunteer so your guests can all play). All players (six or more is best) sit on chairs in a circle, except for the Quiz Master who will call out yes or no questions to the group. The players who answer yes to each question move to the seat on their right, whether that seat is empty or *not!* If they answer no, they stay put. Then the Quiz Master asks another question, and those who answer yes move to the right again—and so on. (Yes, there might be several people sitting on one chair at a time!) The first person to get back to his or her original seat wins!

Here are five saucy questions to get you started:

◾ Do you have a crush on someone in the room?

◾ Have you gone to the bathroom today and not washed your hands afterward?

◾ Have you ever cheated on a test?

CG! tip: If you're not feeling these games, don't worry. There are plenty of other fun activities throughout the different parties (pages 37 to 110). Any of them will make a great icebreaker no matter what theme or kind of party you are throwing. Pick your favorites and have them on hand next time you need to loosen up a crowd.

your party problems **solved**

It's your party and you definitely don't want to be crying at it. A good hostess is prepared for any obstacle. So before you melt into a puddle of tears check out these dilemmas. Then read our expert advice on how to handle sticky situations and get them under control before they turn your party into a pooper.

opposing parties

Q: "My best friend and I had a huge fight. I want her to be at my party, but she won't talk to me and I don't want to be the one to make the first move. What can I do?"

A: Not to make a cheesy party pun here, but you can't have your cake and eat it too! You have to figure out what is more important to you—swallowing your pride and making the first move so you can have your best friend by your side, or standing your ground and going through with your party without her. Only you can decide, but think hard about how you'll feel if she's not there celebrating with you. It won't be the same, plus the party won't be your main focus since you'll be preoccupied thinking about the fight. If you do decide to make the first move and your friend won't take your calls, send her a

well-thought-out e-mail asking her to put your differences aside for the night and come have fun. Let her know how much you'd miss having her there. Once you get together under happy circumstances you may even find the fight completely blows over. But if she doesn't answer your e-mail, don't force it. There will be plenty of other parties and you'll feel better knowing you tried to make things right.

bomb squad

Q: "The last party I had was a total bomb. No one danced and nobody seemed like they were having fun. Everyone just kind of hung around looking bored. Now I'm afraid to have another one, even though I love having people over."

A: Every hostess wants her party to be a super success, but that can create a lot

of pressure for things to be perfect. If you're nervous or can't relax, your guests sometimes pick up on that. The more fun you have at your own party, the more fun everyone else will have too. So grab one of your friends and be the first to show off your moves on the dance floor. It also helps to plan ahead. Make a party mix of your favorite upbeat songs or ask friends to bring their iPods so you can have tons of music options. And think of one or two games or activities you'd like to play. (You'll find lots of ideas in this book!) Getting people involved rather then just sitting around is a sure way to guarantee your party will be a hit.

cheat sheet

Q: "I was taking a bag of trash out during my party and when I opened the door to the garage I walked in on one of my friends kissing my boyfriend! I blew up at them, my party ended up breaking up sooner then it was supposed to, and I spent the rest of the night in tears. Help!"

A: Seeing that is enough to make you want to start World War 3. And rightly so! You trusted two people who were supposed to be close to you and they not only betrayed that trust, but they did it on your turf during your special night! Of course, you can't go back in time and have a "re-do" of the party. But if something like this (or something

---

☺ CG! ouch: pasty complexion!

❝ I was friends with the sister of this guy I liked, and she asked me to come to her slumber party. I was the first one to fall asleep, so my friends played the typical slumber-party trick on me and outlined my face with toothpaste. The next morning I was walking toward the bathroom, not knowing what they'd done, and her brother was just walking out. I smiled, started to make small talk with him, and was really psyched—that is until I looked in the mirror and saw the toothpaste all over my face. I was so embarrassed and I couldn't look the guy in the eye for the rest of the day!"

else just as upsetting) happens again, here's the plan. Although it's hard, the best thing to do is deal with the situation later. Do whatever you need to do to remain calm (count to ten, go scream into a pillow, etc.), then as nicely as possible, ask them to leave quietly and tell them you'd prefer to figure it out tomorrow. A true hostess never lets anything ruffle her feathers, so be the bigger person, keep your cool, and go back to hosting your fabulous party. It will drive your boyfriend and friend crazy, since it's not the expected reaction and they'll soon be begging for your forgiveness.

drama queen

Q: "My best friend broke up with her boyfriend during my birthday party, made a huge scene, and then got hysterical. Crying, she dragged me upstairs to my bedroom and made me stay with her half the night so I missed most of my party. I wanted to be there for her, but I left all my guests waiting downstairs—and gossiping about the whole show. What should I have done?"

A: It's tough when something bad happens right in the middle of something good. You're torn between wanting to feel sad for your friend and wanting to be happy about your celebration. And that's completely normal. Next time someone gets upset or overly dramatic during your party, quickly

CG! tip: You may be too nervous or busy during the party to eat the fabulous food you're serving. But you don't want to lose your juice half way through the festivities. Make sure to chow down on a pre-party power snack about 45 minutes before guests arrive. It will keep your energy up so you can party on down! Try:

- Half a turkey sandwich on whole grain bread
- English muffin pizza with veggies
- Fruit-flavored yogurt drink
- Apple slices with peanut butter

bring her to a quiet place away from the crowd. If she stays in the party room, she might play up the drama for the audience and try to get others involved—which will make for a memorable party, but not in a good way! Once you're both alone, let her cry or vent for five or ten minutes. After that, if she won't let you leave be honest but supportive. Tell her how sad you are about what happened and that you want to talk more, but you also have an obligation to your other guests. If she won't come back to the party with you, suggest another friend who can sit with her in the meantime, then see if she'd want to spend the night so you can give her your undivided attention after everyone else has left.

fashion front and center

How you look can be just as important as the food, fun, and games of your party!

scene stealer

It's your night, so don't be afraid to look the part. These guidelines will help you dress to impress for every occasion.

---

the look: *Glam*

perfect for: Formal affair, dinner party, holiday party, Oscar night, Saturday night mixer

glam: Sparkly tank and sexy skinny jeans, LBD (little black dresses!), fitted blazer and sequined scarf, strappy sandals, metallic accessories, one bold animal print piece, red lips, smoky dark liner

not glam: Over-the-top cleavage, anything too tight, visible panty lines, head-to-toe sequins, glitter, or shine

---

the look: *Girlie*

perfect for: Birthday brunch, tea party, summer evening soiree

girlie: Flirty sundress, denim mini, lacey tank, pastels, sweet prints (i.e.: polka dots, hearts, or mini flowers), ballet flats, embellished flat sandals, headband, loose chignon, pink blush, shimmery lip gloss

not girlie: Girlie hair (i.e., pigtails) *and* girlie clothes—pick one or the other; head to toe lace, frills, ruffles, or bows

the look: *Hippie Chic*

perfect for: Casual Friday hangout, coffee house night, girl's night

hippie chic: Ethnic print tunic, fitted army jacket over flowy dress, faux fur vest, dark leggings, hoop earrings, layered necklaces and bold rings, cute headscarf, ankle boots

not hippie chic: Oversized top with oversized bottom, hole-y jeans, combat boots, hairy pits (ew!), unbrushed hair

the look: *Outdoorsy*

perfect for: Pool party, backyard BBQ

outdoorsy: Layered tank, graphic tee, printed capris, cropped jeans, slip-on sneakers, embellished flip flops, bikini with cute matching sarong, fun costume jewelry (i.e.: chunky Lucite bangles, colorful beaded necklaces, or kitschy charm bracelets)

not outdoorsy: Jog bra or other workout clothes, too-skimpy bikini, visible bra straps, micro-shorts, heavy makeup, fussy hair

guest alert: dress code decoded

It's getting harder and harder to decipher invitation dress codes. Smart casual? Casual chic? Semi-formal? Who can tell what these things mean? And it seems like there are new categories popping up all the time. If you're unsure, don't hesitate to call and ask the hostess what other people might be wearing. It's better to double check then show up in something that will make you uncomfortable all night.

CG! fashion editors **spill**

smart style ideas from people you trust!

" A simple black dress can be perfect for any occasion, but the accessories are what make or break the outfit. So have fun with them, but remember less is more! The general rule is to take off the last accessory you put on and then you'll be wearing just the right amount!**"**

" When you are the hostess you want to look stylish, but since you'll be standing and moving around a lot you also want to be comfortable. So don't go for the highest heels, pick a medium height. And if you opt for a dress, steer clear of minis for the night. Otherwise, if you drop something, how are you going to bend down without flashing your cheeks to everyone!?**"**

" It's always important to remember the hostess sets the tone, even when it comes to the dress code. If you host your party barefoot, you create a casual, laid-back atmosphere and your guests are signaled to make themselves right at home. Let your clothes set the example and others will follow.**"**

" If you'll be cooking or serving food, try to wear something close fitting and avoid anything with drapey sleeves or long, dangling accessories that might dip into the food—or worse, catch fire at the stove. Also consider wearing darker colors that will camouflage any spills or splashes.**"**

" Hostessing can be a very messy business, so be sure to wear something that you aren't afraid to get dirty or something that can be cleaned if it does.**"**

" House parties are a great time, particularly if you're a guest, to test-drive looks that could be problematic when you're at a club or out—like a pair of high stilettos (you can always slip them off when you're at your friend's if they start to hurt) or a floaty dress that could blow up unexpectedly when you're outdoors.**"**

" Fashion is the centerpiece of a great party! Go all out and throw events where dressing up is the whole point, like a masquerade night, a red-carpet Oscar party, or a designer-theme party where guests have to come in their favorite designer duds.**"**

hostess with the **mostess**

countdown to **pretty**!

If you want to make a fashion splash, start prepping at least a week or so before your party.

two weeks before

If you're planning on a haircut or coloring, make the appointment at least two weeks before the big event.

the week before

■ Go through your closet and figure out what you want to wear. Make sure the outfit you choose doesn't need cleaning or fixing and that you have all the accessories you need to go with it. Hit the mall if you need (or want!) to pick up something special or new.

two to three days before

■ Give yourself (or get) a mani-pedi. Make sure to apply topcoat so you won't chip when you're busy in the kitchen making snacks and drinks.

■ Do any other special beauty treatments you might want, like a facial, eyebrow wax, or deep conditioner.

■ If you want a golden glow, apply self tanner a few days before. You'll want to do it in advance so any streaks have a chance to fade.

one day before

■ Claim the 'loo. You'll probably want to take a little extra time getting ready for your special event, so make sure to alert your family when and for how long you'll want access to the bathroom on the day of the party. That way they can work around your schedule and you can stay calm and collected while you primp.

■ Sleep tight: Get a full eight hours of beauty rest so you can wake up alert and attractive!

three or four hours before

Shower and do your hair and makeup. Plan accordingly so you are completely finished at least an hour and a half before the party starts.

30 to 45 minutes before

■ Get dressed and accessorized. If you plan to work in the kitchen after, make sure to cover up with an apron—but remove it before guests arrive.

■ Get psyched! Play your party mix and practice your runway strut in front of the mirror.

15 minutes before

Reapply gloss, flip your hair, pour yourself some punch, and chill out until the fun begins.

CG! dare: Your party is the perfect time to try out a new look. Experiment for the night with something you'd never go to school in, like graphic neon eyeliner or temporary funky colored streaks in your hair. As hostess, it's okay to stand out a little, so don't be afraid to make one bold statement with your outfit.

CG! tip: **CREATE A PARTY OUTFIT FLIPBOOK.** Spend one rainy weekend putting together several different outfits, including accessories and shoes, that would work for a variety of party situations. Try them on and have someone take a picture of you in each one. Save the photos in a book or in a folder on your computer and next time you're knee deep in your closet crying that you have nothing to wear, just consult your flipbook and you'll be party perfect in no time flat.

notes

3-2-1 **party!**

3-2-1 party!

Put on your party pants, sister, it's time to get your groove on. We've got 20 amazing themes that will turn your house into an A-list hot spot. Big or small, indoors or outdoors, casual or dressy, you'll find all kinds of ways to celebrate holidays, birthdays, or just Fridays. And with detailed how-tos for everything

from yummy snacks to unforgettable invites, pulling it all together will be a piece of...well, cake! So hurry up and turn the page because life is a party waiting to happen and you should be the one throwing it!

chocoholics **unite**!

Do you really need an excuse to eat chocolate? Heck, no! So bring your friends over to the dark side for a night of chocolate-making madness. $$$

SET THE MOOD!
chocolate invites

Give your guests the golden ticket to your party. Here's how: Cut out small squares of gold foil paper. Write the party details in marker on each square. Fold the paper in half with the gold side facing out. Slip the paper in between the label and silver foil wrapping of a candy bar. Make sure the tip of it sticks out a little so you see a hint of gold. Then, hand out the candy bars to your invitees.

EAT!
create a chocolate bar

This impressive centerpiece is easy to make—and even easier to eat!

1. Cover your table in layers of translucent colored cellophane.

2. Place a chocolate fountain in the center. There are all different kinds of fountains available. Follow the directions carefully for setting it up. No fountain? Swap in a fondue set—ask Mom, she might already have one buried in the back of the kitchen cabinets!

3. Fill assorted bowls with yummy dipping options (see "Dippity Do!") and arrange them all around the fountain.

4. Remove the labels from several large candy bars and tape them neatly around two tall glass vases. Fill the vases with long wooden skewers ($4/pack, at party stores) and place them on either side of the fountain or fondue pot so guests can use them to spear food.

EAT!
dippity do!

Dip any (or all!) of these tasty tidbits into the chocolate fountain or fondue pot.

- Oreos
- marshmallows
- Twinkies (cut into slices)
- pretzels
- graham crackers
- glazed donut holes
- Rice Krispie treats
- strawberries

cocoa loco confessional!

Before you pig out, let everyone know the Rule of the Chocolate Fountain: Anytime someone lets a goody slip off a skewer and fall into the chocolate, they must confess their most sinfully dark secret to the group!

CG! tip: Although the night is all about chocolate, you want to avoid a cocoa overload—or the festivities may end sooner then you'd like! Have plenty of ice cold milk on hand to wash things down and a few savory items like chips or mini pizza rolls so guests can balance out their sugar high.

CHOCOLATE RULES!

chocolate factory

ONCE YOU'VE HAD YOUR FILL OF THE FOUNTAIN, GATHER YOUR FRIENDS AROUND THE KITCHEN TABLE FOR THE MAIN EVENT: CHOCOLATE MAKING! IN JUST A FEW SIMPLE STEPS YOU CAN CREATE AMAZING GOURMET-STYLE CONFECTIONS.

SUPPLIES

- assorted shaped chocolate molds
- cooking spray
- chocolate melting wafers in assorted flavors (white, milk, dark, etc.)
- toppings such as sprinkles, crushed peanuts, shredded coconut, decorating sugar, mini M&Ms, and other assorted goodies

1. Lightly coat the candy molds with a small amount of cooking spray. This will help keep the candy from sticking.

CG! tip: Don't want to use the molds? Dip some of the food in the fountain (like Oreos or pretzels), cover them in sprinkles or other decorations, and freeze them as you would the molds.

2. Place the chocolate wafers in small microwaveable bowls. (Make sure to separate the different types of chocolate into separate bowls). Microwave 1 bowl of chocolate for 30 seconds and stir. Continue melting at 15 second intervals, checking and stirring in between until it's creamy and spoonable. Don't let it heat for too long or it will get too liquidy.

3. When it's ready, pour or spoon chocolate into one of the molds. Be careful—the bowl might be hot so use oven mitts to carry it to the table. Fill each of the openings in one mold tray almost to the top. Then tap the tray gently against the table to remove any air bubbles.

4. Sprinkle toppings over the chocolate. Place the mold in the freezer for about 10 minutes.

5. Repeat steps 1 through 4 until all the guests have had a chance to fill their molds and decorate their chocolates.

6. When the chocolate is set, turn the mold upside down, gently flex it, and press down on the back to release the candy pieces. They should pop out fairly easily. If not, place the mold back in the freezer for another few minutes until the chocolate has hardened completely.

mad cap "tee" party

Need a break from reality? This fantasy tee-shirt party is the answer, so get ready to fall down the rabbit hole and let the creativity (and the tea!) start to flow. $$$

SET THE MOOD!

balloon party popper invites

SUPPLIES
- colored paper
- balloons
- confetti
- funnel
- ribbon
- Sharpie pen

1. Write the party details on colorful squares of paper. If you can't provide tees, make sure to include a note asking guests to bring a plain white tee or tank.

2. Fold a square of paper several times and insert into a balloon. Add a handful of confetti, using a funnel to guide it into the balloon. Carefully blow up the balloon and tie a knot. Tie a length of curling ribbon to the end (double knot it around the end of the balloon so it's secure) so you can carry the balloons by the string. Repeat with all the balloons and invitations.

3. Using a Sharpie, very gently write "POP ME" on each balloon. Tie a balloon on the door of each friend's house or hand them out in person. When your guests pop the balloons they'll be showered with confetti and the folded invite!

MAKE IT YOURSELF!

tee-rific workspace

Start the party off with the tee-making activity. Here's how to create a magical workspace that will inspire creativity.

■ Cover the table in butcher block paper. It will protect your workspace and your guests can doodle on it and sketch out their designs beforehand.

■ Drape each chair in different colored and patterned fabric (raid the scrap bin or discount table at your local fabric store). To hold the fabric in place, tie on a coordinating colored ribbon and make a large bow at the back of the chair.

■ Hang several feather boas from the ceiling around the table to create a crazy "car-wash" effect. Bonus: Invite guests to pull off feathers to glue onto their tees if they want.

■ Arrange a little bouquet of tea roses (mini roses) in a cute teapot to make a centerpiece. Scatter some of the rose petals around the table or place a few buds in teacups.

■ Divide up supplies (rhinestones, buttons, sequins, etc.) on mix-n-match paper plates. Don't forget fabric glue, fabric markers, scissors, measuring tapes, pencils, and needle and thread.

tee time!

Here are some ideas for five nifty tees to get your crafty juices flowing.

sequin tank

Using fabric glue or a hot-glue gun, glue large paillettes (flat sequins with a hole in the top instead of the center) in horizontal rows, overlapping each paillette until the front of the straps and the top third of the tank top are covered. If you used fabric glue, let dry flat for several hours.

bow tank

Hot-glue (or fabric glue) 3-inch-wide black crochet trim along the neckline. Make a bow using 25 inches of trim, leaving the ends long. Hot-glue bow to center of collar. Let dry.

pom-pom tank

Hot-glue (or fabric glue) sequin trim around the neckline, then add pom-pom trim below the sequins and along armholes. Knot 2 mini tassels around the center pom-pom. Let dry.

word tank

Use a fabric marker to cover a white tee-shirt with your favorite phrase or words in diagonal rows. Cut off the sleeves to make a tank. Then cut a 1-inch strip of fabric from one of the sleeves, make a bow and sew it to the front at the neckline.

rhinestone tee

Layout gemstones in a "necklace" shape starting 3 inches below the tee's shoulder seams. Carefully hot-glue them in place. Cut a yard of 1-inch-wide ribbon in half. Turn edge of one end under ½ inch and hot-glue it down to form hem. Hot-glue hemmed end of ribbon directly above rhinestones on one side. Repeat with other piece of ribbon on the other side. Tie the ends of the two ribbons at the back of your neck in a bow.

project tee-shirt

Near the end of the party, model your creations for each other. Then vote on the best designs and give prizes to the winners. Don't worry about favors since everyone gets to take home their brand new tee!

EAT!
tea time menu

While your tees are drying, take a break for some sweet treats and elegant snacks.

■ Tea sandwiches: Make your favorite sandwiches (try chicken salad, egg salad, or even PB and J) and use cookie cutters to cut them into fun shapes.

■ Pastel colored Jordan almonds and candy mints.

■ Assorted petit-fours and mini cakes (à la *Alice in Wonderland*!): Pick up at your local bakery.

■ Scrumptious Sorbets.

■ Selection of teas: Serve with sugar, lemon, and milk.

EAT!

scrumptious sorbet

raspberry sorbet

INGREDIENTS

- 3 cups simple syrup
- 3 tablespoons fresh lemon juice (about 1 lemon)
- 5 cups fresh or frozen raspberries
- 1 cup water
- mint leaves
- raspberries

MAKES ABOUT 6 SERVINGS

1. Combine the syrup, lemon juice, raspberries, and water in a large bowl. Divide into two equal portions. Blend one portion in a blender on high until smooth. Remove excess seeds by straining the mixture through a fine mesh strainer into a large bowl. Repeat with the other portion. Transfer to a plastic storage container and chill for at least 2 hours.

2. Pour the mixture into an ice cream maker and follow the manufacturers' directions for the machine. Scoop into serving dishes and garnish each with mint leaves and a raspberry.

simple syrup

Bring 2 cups sugar and 2 cups water to a boil in a saucepan over medium-high heat. Cook, stirring frequently, for about 6 minutes, or until the sugar is completely dissolved. Let syrup cool before using.

CG! soiree swap:

This party also makes a unique birthday celebration. Crown the guest of honor with a sparkly tiara and have everyone collaborate to make her a special birthday tee.

CG! tip: If you don't have an ice cream maker, pour the mixture into a 12-inch square cake pan and place in the freezer. Stir every 15 minutes until slushy. Transfer to a plastic container and freeze for at least 6 hours.

3-2-1 party!

45

sunrise
surprise party

Wake your friend up CG! style and kidnap her for a super surprise party that rocks harder than her iPod alarm clock! $

SET THE MOOD!
birthday blog invites

Set up a party website or blog so you can post notes to guests and work together on scheduling and planning the big kidnap. (Make sure to talk to your friend's parents first to get their permission—and help.) Send the link out as the invite, then ask guests to create party profiles and write tributes to the birthday girl. At the end of the party, upload photos of the event onto the page and share the link with your friend so she can have a virtual memory book.

EAT!
menu: breakfast buffet bonanza

It's the best meal of the day so go all out. Set up a buffet with lots of choices, such as:

■ Mini waffles with ice cream (waffle sandwiches!).

■ French toast sticks with different dipping syrups.

■ Juice bar with assorted flavors.

■ Birthday Breakfast Burritos: Have your guests create their own.

■ Assorted cereals: Place in clear canisters with labels.

RISE AND SHINE!

EAT!
birthday breakfast burritos

CG! tip: You may want to enlist your mom or dad to make the eggs while you are out picking up the birthday girl so they'll be ready when you get back.

INGREDIENTS
- 2 dozen eggs
- ½ cup milk
- salt and pepper to taste
- butter for frying
- assorted fillings: shredded cheeses (mozzarella, Monterey Jack, Cheddar), salsa, chopped sautéed onions and peppers, sour cream, etc.
- 12 to 15 flour tortillas

MAKES 12 TO 15 SERVINGS.

1. In a large bowl, whisk the eggs with the milk and salt and pepper for 2 to 3 minutes. You may want to do 6 or 7 eggs at a time so it doesn't get too overwhelming.

2. Melt butter in a 12-inch frying pan over medium heat. Once the butter is almost completely melted and starts to sizzle, add ⅓ cup of the egg mixture. Let it sit for about 30 seconds, then begin to scramble using a spatula or flat spoon. Cook, scrambling, until the eggs are just set. Transfer to a large bowl. Repeat with remaining eggs.

3. Place the bowl of eggs in the center of the table along with bowls of salsa, cheese, veggies, and other fillings or toppings. Give each guest a tortilla and let her create a burrito to her liking.

EAT!
ice cream cake

WHO CARES IF IT'S BREAKFAST—IT WOULDN'T BE A BIRTHDAY PARTY WITHOUT CAKE!

INGREDIENTS
- 1 (18.25-ounce) box standard chocolate cake mix
- 3 eggs
- 1 pint Ben & Jerry's Chocolate Fudge Brownie Ice Cream, softened
- 2 cups (one 12-ounce bag) semisweet chocolate chips
- 1 (16-ounce) tub vanilla frosting
- 1 (2-ounce) jar colored sprinkles

1. Preheat the oven to 350°F. Grease the bottom of a 13x9-inch baking dish. In a large bowl, mix the cake mix, eggs, and ice cream with an electric mixer on medium setting for about 2 minutes. Stir in the chocolate chips.

2. Pour the cake batter into the pan. Bake 35 to 40 minutes. Check by sticking in a toothpick after 35 minutes. The cake is done when the toothpick comes out clean. Let cool for 3 hours. Frost the cake, decorate with sprinkles, and refrigerate until ready to serve.

3-2-1 party!

47

kidnap alternatives

■ Don't feel like cooking? Take your kidnapped pal to the local breakfast place—all wearing your PJs!

■ Make it breakfast in bed. Wake up your friend and surprise her, but instead of taking her somewhere serve her breakfast in bed while all the guests eat in the room and have a "morning" slumber party.

■ If it's your party, surprise all your guests by waking *them* up (this takes more work since it's not just one person and you'll have to coordinate with all their parents—but it's worth the look on your friends' faces as you steal them away for your big day!)

■ Ditch the morning idea and invite all your friends over one night for a Breakfast for Dinner party.

special touch

Can't find a cool cake topper? Use a personal trinket that reflects the b-day girl's personality like a sparkly tiara or something quirky like a plastic hula doll.

☺ CG! ouch: **what a boob!**

❝ We were at my friend's slumber party, looking at one of her brother's *Playboy* magazines. I thought that one of the models had fake boobs, so I started going on and on about her lack of nipples. My friends started giggling. I figured they thought I was funny, so I kept talking. Then one of my friends nudged me and I turned around, but since all I saw was the cat, I didn't see any reason to stop ranting. Finally, my friend gave me a weird look, and this time when I turned around, I saw my friend's dad! He had been there the whole time listening to me go on and on about nipples! I was so embarrassed."

hot topics

Find out how well you know your friends with this great conversation starter. Write out interesting questions on colored index cards and place them in a bowl. While you're eating, pass the bowl around so everyone can draw a card. Have each girl read her question. She has to answer it first then go around the table so everyone gets a turn to answer the same question. Keep going until all the cards have been read and answered. Here are some questions to start you off:

■ Who's the weirdest person you've ever had a crush on?

■ What TV character do you relate to the most and why?

■ If you could have a guardian angel who would you choose?

monogrammed pillowcase favors

SUPPLIES
- plain cotton pillowcases (hit the discount bin at home goods stores for cheap sets)
- iron-on letters
- iron
- fabric markers
- ribbon

Customize each pillowcase with a guest's initials. Move the letters around to figure out where you want the monogram to go and then follow the directions on the iron-ons to attach them to the pillowcase. Use fabric markers to decorate around the letters. Roll up each pillowcase and tie with a piece of ribbon.

KIDNAP
BIRTHDAY
BREAKFAST!

poetry slam
coffee house

Invite your friends over for a groovy coffee night, and you can bet they're going to say, "Thanks a latte!" **$$**

puzzle invites

GET THE WORD OUT ABOUT YOUR PARTY WITH THESE PUZZLING INVITES!

SUPPLIES
- blank jigsaw puzzles
- rubber stamps, markers, stickers, or old magazines
- Elmer's Glue-All
- scissors
- paper coffee cups with lids
- permanent marker
- chocolate coffee beans or other coffee-flavored candy

1. Write the details of the party on each assembled blank puzzle. Decorate them with rubber stamps or stickers or cut out letters from old magazines and glue them on for a "ransom letter" look. Let dry.

2. If the coffee cups are plain, neatly write a few lines of your favorite poem, rap, rhyme, or song on them with a marker. Fill each cup about halfway with candy. Break apart a puzzle invite and place the mixed up pieces gently on top of the candy. Cover the cup with the lid and hand out. Repeat with the remaining cups. Guests will have to reassemble the puzzle to get the party scoop. Word!

beatnik décor

Bring the beatnik vibe to your basement with a few simple touches.

Create a poet corner: Designate one section of the room as the "stage" where the poets will perform. Set up a stool or chair in case some performers want to sit and aim a goose-neck desk lamp at the area to create a spotlight. Place pillows and cushions in front of the stage so everyone can sit and watch comfortably.

Go eclectic: Coffee houses usually have a shabby chic mix of furniture so don't worry about it looking perfect. Bring chairs in from all different rooms in your house and decorate with all kinds of patterned pillows. Cover the basement walls with long panels of fabric (alternate solid with print) to make it feel more lounge-y.

Showcase the sweets: So, okay, you probably don't have a glass display case on hand—but you can still make guests feel like they're browsing the baked goods at their local Starbucks by showcasing cupcakes, brownies, or cookies on tiered cake stands or in glass canisters.

Make coffee the centerpiece: Light coffee-scented candles to keep the yummy aroma in the air all night. Fill glass vases with coffee beans instead of water and nestle bouquets of flowers on top. And set up a big coffee bar with all the necessities like sugar, milk, cinnamon, and nutmeg; plus hot water, tea, or cocoa for any non-coffee drinkers.

GROOVY
JAVA DEN!

poetry slam 101

What it is: Simply put, poetry slam is the competitive art of performance poetry. Poets perform their work and are judged by members of the audience on two levels: what they are saying (i.e., the actual content of the poem) and how they are saying it (i.e., the way the poet performs it).

How it usually works: Before the event, poets must prepare an original piece of work. Sometimes a slam will have a theme—like love or the environment or a particular poet whose style you must use as inspiration. Each performer gets 3 minutes (if they go over time they lose points) to perform their poem alone without using props or music but just the sound of their voice and their body movements.

What you can do: Poetry slams can be strict about the rules, but it varies based on the slam so feel free to mix it up and adjust things for your enjoyment. For example, don't feel obligated to write your *own* poems. Instead people can opt to perform another poet's work or even a spoken word version of their favorite song. And if anyone is truly inspired to use silly props or even dress in costume they should go for it!

A few more things: Don't forget to record everyone's performance. It can help with the judging if you can screen instant replays. Plus, it will make a super-fun souvenir when you burn everyone a copy. Elect a few people to be judges or you can all vote on slips of paper. Winner gets a prize (gift certificate to Starbucks, perhaps!?) Still need more guidance? Check out poetryslam.com or search "poetry slam" on YouTube to see some in action.

> **CG! tip:** In between poetry readings, take a break for a musical interlude. Enlist an aspiring musician friend (or two or three!) and ask them to prepare a small set to play.

CG! soiree swap

If music is more your thing, turn this into a laid-back CD- listening party. Next time your favorite band is releasing a new album, invite friends over for the premiere playing and for a little after-listening coffee talk! Instead of the puzzle invite, make a customized CD and burn some greatest hits so guests can get acquainted with your band's style. (See invite from Sweet Sixteen for help, page 54.)

EAT!

chocolate chip espresso cookies

THESE YUM-TASTIC COOKIES WILL GIVE YOU A JOLT OF JAVA—PERFECT FOR KEEPING UP THAT PERFORMANCE ENERGY!

INGREDIENTS

- 2 1/2 cups semisweet chocolate chips
- 4 tablespoons (1/2 stick) unsalted butter
- 2 large eggs
- 3/4 cup granulated sugar
- 1 teaspoon ground espresso or other finely ground dark-roast coffee beans
- 1/4 cup all-purpose flour
- 1/4 teaspoon baking powder
- 1/4 teaspoon salt

MAKES ABOUT 30 COOKIES

1. Bring 2 cups water to a boil in a pot. Lower to a simmer. Put a glass bowl over the pot; add 1 ¾ cups of the chocolate chips and all of the butter; stir constantly until it melts.

2. In a large bowl, whisk the eggs and sugar together until light and fluffy. Stir in the espresso, then mix in the chocolate mixture. Let it cool.

In a small bowl, combine the flour, baking powder, and salt. Stir the flour mixture and the remaining 3/4 cup chocolate chips into the chocolate mixture. Put the bowl in the fridge for 15 to 30 minutes to let the dough firm up. Make tablespoon-sized dough balls and place on a cookie sheet. Freeze the cookie dough overnight.

4. To bake, preheat the oven to 375°F. Completely grease a new cookie sheet. Don't thaw the dough. Arrange the dough balls 2 inches apart on the greased sheet. Bake 7 to 10 minutes, checking to see if they're done by sticking in a toothpick. If it comes out close to clean, they're ready! If it comes out wet with batter, continue to bake the cookies until done. Repeat with the remaining dough balls.

vanilla thrilla frappes

THESE VANILLA BLENDED DRINKS WILL COMPLEMENT THE CHOCOLATE ESPRESSO COOKIES NICELY.

INGREDIENTS

- 4 cups freshly brewed coffee
- 1 cup milk
- 2 scoops vanilla ice cream
- 6 to 8 teaspoons sugar (to taste)
- 1 tablespoon vanilla extract
- 8 to 10 ice cubes

MAKES 5 SERVINGS.

1. Chill the coffee in refrigerator until lukewarm to cool. (Don't let it get cold, though, or the taste can become bitter.) Place the coffee, milk, ice cream, sugar, and vanilla extract in a blender and blend together about 10 seconds, or until slightly foamy. Add a few cubes of ice and blend until the ice is broken up.

2. Repeat until you've used all the ice. Pour into glasses and serve.

Want more of a chocolate fix? Use a half a cup of chocolate syrup in place of the vanilla extract and chocolate ice cream instead of vanilla.

GROOVY JAVA DEN!

sweet sixteen
sit-down

Celebrate your birthday and impress all your friends with this sophisticated (but easy to put together!) dinner party. Cheers! $$$

SET THE MOOD!
playlist invites

SET THE VIBE OF THE PARTY TO COME BY CREATING A PERSONALIZED PLAYLIST, THEN BURN THE SONGS ONTO CDS FOR ALL OF THE GUESTS.

SUPPLIES
- blank CDs in jewel cases
- red paper
- markers
- large red CD envelopes
- round CD labels
- scissors

1. Download 10 or 12 of your favorite songs to create your personal party mix. Burn it onto the blank CDs. Place labels on the CDs, write out the playlist, and decorate.

2. Print out the party info on red paper. Cut to fit in the front of the jewel cases, then slip into the cases.

3. Place each CD in a case and put the whole thing into an envelope. Mail or hand out to friends.

red all over!

■ Create a centerpiece by stacking several white gift boxes and tying them together with red ribbon.

■ Wrap the back of each chair with wide red ribbon.

■ Line one whole wall with red helium balloons.

■ For a modern take on flower arrangements, put red rosebuds on silver trays and in silver cups.

■ Scatter red votive candles all around the table.

EAT!

never-been-kissed menu

Hors d'oeuvres: Spicy Crab Sushi Rolls.

Appetizer: Green salad; buy it prewashed, add your favorite veggies, and toss with dressing.

Entrée: Huge bowl of pasta; get family-style takeout from your favorite Italian restaurant and serve on fancy dishes. We won't tell anyone that you didn't make it!

Dessert: Doughnut Tower.

Drinks: Cherry Lemonade Twists.

EAT!

spicy crab sushi roll

INGREDIENTS
- 3 cups sushi rice
- 1 small cucumber
- 1/2 pound imitation crabmeat
- 1 tablespoon chopped dill
- 1/3 cup wasabi mayonnaise
- 10 sheets rice paper or seaweed wrap (at grocery or health food stores)

MAKES 10 PIECES, ABOUT 15 SERVINGS (2 TO 3 PIECES PER PERSON).

1. Prepare the sushi rice, following directions on the box (you'll need 3 cups). Peel the cucumber, cut in half lengthwise, and spoon out and discard the seeds. Cut the rest into 1/4-inch slices. Combine the cucumber, crab-meat, dill, and wasabi mayonnaise in a large bowl and blend to mix.

2. Place a line of sushi rice across the bottom edge of a piece of rice paper or seaweed wrap. Spread a small scoop of the crab mixture on top of the rice. Neatly roll into a cylinder. Cut the roll into four pieces. Repeat with the remaining 9 wrappers.

CG! soiree swap
Change the color theme to make this a swanky holiday party!

3-2-1 party!

cherry lemonade twists

INGREDIENTS

- ice
- 2 liters Cherry 7UP
- 2 quarts lemonade
- 2 tablespoons lime juice
- 4 tablespoons grenadine (for color)
- 12 to 14 red rock candy sticks
- 1 bag Swedish Fish candy

MAKES 2 PITCHERS, ABOUT 12-14 SERVINGS

1. Fill two large pitchers a quarter of the way full with ice. Fill each three-quarters with Cherry 7UP. Finish each with 1 quart lemonade, 1 tablespoon Rose's Lime Juice, and 2 tablespoons grenadine. Stir well.

2. Pour into glasses. Garnish with red rock candy sticks. Serve drinks on a tray with a side of Swedish Fish candy.

EAT!

doughnut tower

INGREDIENTS

- 36 Krispy Kreme traditional cake doughnuts or any plain doughnuts
- red M&Ms
- Hershey's Kisses
- 6 (16-ounce) tubs chocolate and vanilla frosting (three of each)
- roses

MAKES 36 SERVINGS.

Frost each doughnut, alternating vanilla and chocolate frosting so there's an equal number of each. Top with the M&Ms and kisses. Neatly stack the doughnuts on a three-tier cake tray ($30, at home goods stores). Place rosebuds around the trays to decorate.

gift-box place cards

SUPPLIES
- wrapped candy of your choice
- 2x1x1-inch white cardboard boxes
- red ribbon
- gift tags
- scissors
- markers

1. Place a few pieces of candy in each box. Tie 1/2 yard of ribbon around each box. Write guests' names on gift tags and tuck one tag under each ribbon. Tape down tags if they're slipping.

2. Place a box at each seat at the table.

CG! ouch: big mousse-take

❝ I was at this great party, talking to the hottest guy in my school. We were having the greatest conversation and I was thinking, 'Whoa, he might like me!' I was pretty much dying of happiness. Then he asked if I wanted to try some of his dessert. I asked what kind it was, and he told me that it was chocolate mousse. Well, I screamed 'I love you!' when I meant to say 'I love chocolate mousse.' He looked at me like I was a crazy woman!"

CG! ouch: pass the sugar!

❝ The caterer I was working for had to cater a huge party for this major company, and it was really important to my boss that everything go well. She put me in charge of making the dessert.
The recipe called for sugar, so I put in the recommended amount of sugar and served it. Well, it turns out that I didn't use sugar—I had accidentally used salt! The dessert tasted awful and my boss was really mad!"

souvenir frame favors

SUPPLIES
- digital camera
- color printer
- 6x8-inch notecards
- red photo corners

1. Take lots of photos during the night.

2. Print out one best shot of each guest. (If you don't have a printer, ask your dad to run out to a one-hour photo place midway through the party.)

3. Attach the corners to the front of the cards and slip in photos to create a "frame.."

casual **friday**

Is your brain screaming for a rest? Leave your worries (and your books!) behind and spice up a Friday night with this stress-free shindig. **$$**

SET THE MOOD!
take-out invites

TAKE-OUT CARTONS ARE AN UNEXPECTED (AND CHEAP!) WAY TO DELIVER YOUR PARTY NEWS.

SUPPLIES
- printer paper
- scissors
- take-out cartons
- glue stick
- colored tissue paper
- assorted candy

Jenny & Lisa Invite You To Chill out. Friday, November 18th 7 o'clock in the evening 2233 Autumn Road RSVP to Jenny

1. For each invitation, print out the party info on printer paper. Cut neatly around it so that it fits onto the side of the take-out box. Glue it down smoothly onto the box.

2. Place a few pieces of colored tissue paper inside each box and fluff the top so it sticks out. Fill with a handful of assorted candy. Deliver the boxes to your friends at school.

SET THE MOOD!
de-stress décor

- Pick a soothing color theme, like turquoise and gold.
- Make things comfy with lots of big floor pillows and soft throw blankets.
- Use colored light bulbs to create a cool glow.
- Light scented candles—try sandalwood. (Note: Never leave burning candles unattended!)
- Zen flower bowls: Fill some pretty glass bowls three-quarters full with water. Cut the stems from gardenias and place a few in each bowl to float. Scatter the bowls around the room.

TGIF!

TAKE AWAY!

sweet ending

Use leftover cellophane to wrap up each friend's chocolate masterpieces and tie with a bit of ribbon or string. Then send everyone home to have sweet dreams of the big event.

delicious downloads

- "Candyman," Christina Aguilera
- "The Sweet Escape," Gwen Stefani
- "I Want Candy," Aaron Carter
- "Sugar, Sugar," the Archies
- "Chocolate," Kylie Minogue
- "Sweet Dreams (Are Made of This)," Eurythmics

CHOCOLATE RULES!

❗ CG! party lines:

❝ What is one of the main reasons people love parties? The food! And especially the dessert! That's what everyone always eats so, I decided to have a Candyland-themed party. There were bowls of candy everywhere you looked, an ice cream bar, cupcakes, different sodas, a chocolate fountain, and a testing table where you could try crazy or foreign candies. There was also a large board where everyone wrote down their favorite candy. The decorations were in pinks and purples, yellows, and bright blues and greens. Candy was hung from the ceiling, and lollipop trees decorated the floor just like a wonderland of sugar! Everyone let loose and pigged out and it was a great night!"

—Taylor, San Francisco, CA

EAT!
mellow-out menu

Snack: Mini Gourmet Grilled Cheese Sandwiches, plus mini hot dogs and mini hamburgers (cut regular ones into bite-sized pieces); with assorted dipping sauces (ketchup, flavored mustards, BBQ sauce, etc.)

Drink: Citrus Fruit Spritzers

Sweet Treat: Frozen Hot Chocolate

EAT!
mini gourmet grilled cheese sandwiches

INGREDIENTS

- 3 to 4 tablespoons vegetable oil
- 1 loaf white bread
- 1 loaf sourdough bread
- 10 slices Cheddar cheese
- 10 slices American cheese
- 1 bag shredded Monterey Jack cheese

MAKES 40 MINI SANDWICHES.

1. Heat 1 tablespoon of the vegetable oil in a medium skillet over medium heat for 3 minutes. Place 2 slices of white bread in the pan and cook for 3 to 4 minutes, or until the bottoms are light brown.

2. Put 1 slice of Cheddar and 1 slice of American cheese, plus a handful of Monterey Jack, on 1 slice of bread. Cover with the other slice of bread and press down with back of a spatula. Continue cooking, turning once, until both sides are golden brown and the cheese is melted. Remove the sandwich from the skillet.

3. Use the remaining bread and cheese to make 9 more sandwiches, alternating between white and sourdough bread for variety. Add another tablespoon of vegetable oil to the skillet every other time you make another sandwich.

4. Cut each sandwich diagonally both ways to create 4 mini sandwiches.

frozen hot chocolate

INGREDIENTS
- 1 (6-ounce) package Serendipity 3 Secret Frrrozen Hot Chocolate mix ($15/3 packages, serendipity3.com)
- 1 cup milk
- 3 cups ice
- whipped cream
- grated chocolate

MAKES 2 LARGE FROZEN HOT CHOCOLATES, SERVING 2 TO 3.

1. Place the packaged mix, milk, and ice in a large blender. Blend on medium speed until thick and creamy.

2. Pour into a large glass bowl and place in the freezer for 20 minutes before serving for a super-cold kick! Garnish with tons of whipped cream and grated chocolate.

3. Add a bunch of straws and spoons and invite guests to gather round and share! Yum!

DRINK!
citrus fruit spritzers

For each spritzer, mix 1/4 cup Snapple pink lemonade and 3/4 cup Island Fruit 7UP Plus in a shaker with 3 or 4 ice cubes. Place pineapple-flavored sugar on a small dish. Wet the rim of a glass and turn it upside down, pressing it into the candy on the dish to coat it. Pour the spritzer into the candy-rimmed glass. Repeat for each guest.

TGIF!

TAKE AWAY!
candy-to-go favors

Splurge on some candy-filled lunch boxes for truly impressive party favors. Or, if you'd like to go DIY: Fill mini lunch boxes with your favorite candy. Write guests' names on paper tags and attach to the boxes with ribbon.

> ## ❗ CG! party lines
>
> " What I've found really works is being original. Although you may have been to some really cool parties that you loved, it won't be special if you do the same thing for yours. Plus no one likes to do the same thing twice. Follow through with your own ideas and don't be embarrassed to use them. Make your party your own party, not someone else's. For my bat mitzvah, my theme was Under the Sea because I love to sail. I had real fish swimming in the flower vases, and we had "mermaid dancers" come out. Doing things like that is what will make the party great so don't be afraid to be original."
>
> —Sabina, New York, NY

> ## 😲 CG! ouch: daring daughter!
>
> " It was my best friend's birthday and the first coed party I'd ever been to. We decided to play truth or dare, and I went first. My crush dared me to run down the street without a shirt on. Being the daredevil that I am, I did it. I went out the back door and began my adventure. I was halfway down the street when I saw a red car coming over the hill. It was my father coming to pick me up—and there I was shirtless and standing a block away from my friend's house! I ran back to the house, got my shirt, and got in the car really fast. I tried to explain everything to my dad, but he didn't seem to want to hear it. Let me tell you something—I'll never do that again!"

snow **ball**

No wearing glass slippers to *this* shindig! Break out your boots and host a New Year's Eve *après ski* party that rocks so hard it just may start an avalanche! **$$**

trail map invites

GET THE WINTRY THEME GOING FROM THE START!

SUPPLIES

- ski trail map (print out from online)
- scissors
- construction paper
- Elmer's Glue-All
- 2 yards 1/8-inch-wide silver ribbons
- snowflake confetti
- 9x9-inch envelopes

1. On a color copier, blow up the ski map 150 percent and print out copies. Cut the maps into 7x12-inch rectangles. Fold in half with the map on the outside to form cards.

2. Cut 6x7-inch rectangles from construction paper (different colors). Glue two of them inside each card. Print the party info out, cut into strips, and glue on the right side.

3. Glue ribbon around the front edges of the cards. Sprinkle some snow confetti in each envelope and add a card. Hand deliver to all your guests.

HAPPY NEW YEAR!

EAT!
popcorn s'mores

INGREDIENTS

- 1 cup firmly packed light brown sugar
- 1/2 cup (1 stick) butter
- 1/2 cup corn syrup
- 1/2 teaspoon baking soda
- 10 cups plain popcorn
- 1 (10 1/2-ounce) bag mini-marshmallows
- 2 cups chocolate Teddy Grahams cookies
- 1 (6-ounce package) milk chocolate chips (1 cup)

MAKES 20 SERVINGS.

1. Grease a 9x13-inch baking pan. Combine the brown sugar, butter, and corn syrup in a medium saucepan. Cook over medium heat, stirring occasionally, for 5 minutes, or until the sugar is dissolved. Remove from the heat and stir in the baking soda.

2. Combine the popcorn and marshmallows in a large bowl. Pour the sugar mixture over them and stir to spread it evenly around. (Careful, the mixture is hot!) Stir in the cookies and chocolate chips. Spread the mixture evenly into the prepared pan. Refrigerate 2 hours to cool. Break the s'mores into bite-sized pieces to serve.

ö CG! ouch: love seat!

" My boyfriend and I wanted to spend New Year's Eve together. Well, my mom loves him, so when I asked her if he could come with us to the two parties we were going to, she said yes. She also suggested that he spend the night at our house because she didn't want to drive him home at two o'clock in the morning. My dad wasn't thrilled with this idea (whose father would be?), so he decided to sleep on the pullout couch with my boyfriend! When I went downstairs in the morning, I was horrified to find my dad with his face much too close to my boyfriend's face! It's a good thing that my guy has a sense of humor. Plus, once I was past the embarrassment, the whole situation made for a hilarious story to tell my dad's friends."

EAT!
sweet 'n' spicy cocoa

INGREDIENTS
- 30 (1-ounce) bars semisweet baking chocolate, broken into medium pieces
- peel of 1 medium orange, cut into pieces
- 2 1/2 teaspoon ground cinnamon
- 1 gallon milk
- 1 can whipped cream
- grated semisweet chocolate for garnish (grate it from some of the above chocolate and put it aside until the end instead of melting it)
- cinnamon sticks, for garnish

MAKES 12-14 SERVINGS.

1. Combine the chocolate pieces, orange peel, ground cinnamon, and 2 cups milk in a large saucepan. Heat on medium for 20 to 25 minutes, adding 1 cup of milk every 2 minutes and stirring until the chocolate completely melts.

2. Add the remaining milk (about 2 cups) and heat on medium, stirring often, for about 5 minutes, or until the cocoa is piping hot and steam starts to rise.

3. Carefully pour the cocoa into individual mugs. Top each one with a dollop of whipped cream, a sprinkle of grated chocolate, and a cinnamon stick.

PLAY!
pop secret!

IT'S A RACE TO FIND OUT WHO YOUR NEW YEAR'S EVE KISS IS GOING TO BE!

SUPPLIES
- 6 packs plain white balloons
- scissors
- 15 to 20 sheets white printer paper
- confetti

1. Cut out a paper snowflake for each female guest (including yourself!).

2. Write one girl's name on each snowflake. Fold it up, stick it in a balloon, and blow up the balloon. Repeat until each girl has a balloon with her name in it.

3. Blow up the rest of the balloons without names. Sprinkle all of the balloons with confetti and use to decorate the room to give it a "snow-covered" vibe. Fifteen minutes before midnight, tell the guys to pop balloons until they find one with a name—that girl will be his midnight kiss!

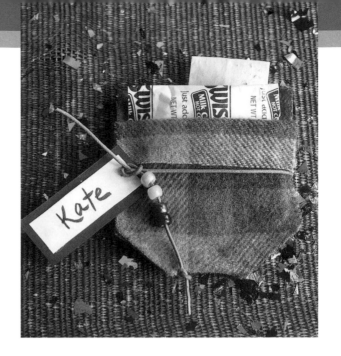

TAKE AWAY!

hot pockets favors

A TREAT THAT KEEPS THE WARM VIBES OF YOUR PARTY GOING ON LONG AFTER YOUR FRIENDS ARE GONE!

SUPPLIES
- flannel fabric scraps
- scissors
- hot-glue gun
- hot cocoa packets
- hand warmers
- colored paper
- leather cord
- colored beads

1. For each favor, cut two equal-sized pocket shapes from the flannel. Hot-glue the edges together, leaving an opening at the top. Tuck a cocoa packet and a hand warmer inside.

2. Make name tags from the paper. Poke a small hole in a tag with scissors. Thread some cord through and tie around the pouch and knot. Put beads on one end and knot. Repeat for all guests. Hand out favors as they leave.

HAPPY NEW YEAR!

groundhog **day party**

On February 2 each year, a little furball looks for his shadow. Who can think of a better reason to party? **$$**

e-invites

Go to the postcard section of punxsutawneyphil.com to electronically invite friends (pick from fun images, like this guy!) to an early morning breakfast party to see the famous Punxsutawney Phil pop up after sunrise. If he doesn't see his shadow, we get an early spring!

punxsutawney punch

Legend has it that Phil drinks a magic punch that lets him live forever! Well, our version isn't magic, but it tastes just great with groundhog-shaped pancakes.

INGREDIENTS

- 2 3/4 cups apple juice
- 1 1/4 cups orange juice
- 1 tablespoon lemon juice
- 2 tablespoons honey
- 2 teaspoons ground cinnamon
- cinnamon sticks, for garnish

MAKES ABOUT 4 SERVINGS.

In a large saucepan, heat the apple juice and orange juice over medium heat until steaming but not boiling. Remove from the heat. Stir in the lemon juice, honey, and ground cinnamon. Pour into mugs and garnish with cinnamon sticks. Mmm!

EAT!
"eat your phil" pancakes

INGREDIENTS
- 1 large egg
- 1 cup milk
- 2 tablespoons vegetable oil
- 1 cup flour
- 1 tablespoon granulated sugar
- 1 tablespoon baking powder
- 1/2 teaspoon salt
- 1 to 2 tablespoons butter
- chocolate chips
- confectioners' sugar
- maple syrup or jam

MAKES ABOUT 6 SERVINGS.

1. Blend the egg, milk, and oil in a medium bowl. Blend the flour, granulated sugar, baking powder, and salt in a large bowl. Add the egg mixture and mix well with a whisk.

2. Grease a skillet with some of the butter and heat over medium-high heat. Pour 1/4 cups of the batter onto the heated skillet, repeat leaving at least an inch of space between each pancake. Cook, turning once, until both sides are golden brown. Repeat with the remaining butter and batter.

3. Place the pancakes on a cookie sheet and use a cookie cutter to cut out a groundhog shape. Add chocolate chips for eyes! Sprinkle with confectioners' sugar and serve with syrup or jam.

PLAY!
tune in

Watch the festivities from Punxsutawney, Pennsylvania (check local listings), while you eat. Phil appears around 7:25 a.m. (Eastern Time) for his big moment to tell us if spring is near! Before you watch, have your friends write down a guess for the number of times the reporters will say "Phil" or "shadow." Then keep count and give a prize to whoever comes closest!

TAKE AWAY!
phil to go

See friends off with hilarious groundhog cupcakes that'll keep the festive mood going even if six more weeks of winter lie ahead. Go to familyfun.com and search for "groundhog cupcake" for the recipe. Make the cupcakes the night before so they are ready to go in the morning.

LONG WINTER OR EARLY SPRING?

girl's only
valentine's

Who says V-day love has to be for a guy? Not you, CosmoGIRL! So gather your best friends for a supersized girl's night. **$$**

SET THE MOOD!
"bee" my valentine invites

Remember those adorable cards with silly puns you used to exchange with every single kid in your class? Go old-school—buy a pack or two of your favorites and write the party details around the pre-printed Valentine's Day message. Don't forget to seal each one with a cute heart sticker and a kiss—SWAK!

SET THE MOOD!
heart-felt décor

■ Fill the room with lots of comfy throw pillows, floor cushions, and blankets for everyone to snuggle up with while you're bonding.

■ Display favorite photos of you and your girls all around to remind everyone how many wonderful memories you've made together.

■ Make a quick and colorful candy centerpiece: Layer jellybeans in glass vases or jars—start with a thick row of dark pink, then a thick row of medium pink, and then light pink to create a striped effect. Repeat with another jar

HAPPY V-DAY!

of red jellybeans and one of pink and white ones. Place on a coffee table and scatter pink, white, and red tea lights around.

■ Don't forget little bowls of candy hearts so you can exchange "love notes" with your g-friends.

EAT!
chick mix

WHO NEEDS BOYS WHEN YOU CAN FALL IN LOVE WITH THIS AMAZINGLY ADDICTIVE PARTY MIX? BETTER STOCK UP—WE GUARANTEE IT'S GOING TO GO FAST.

INGREDIENTS
- 10 ounces mini pretzels
- 5 cups Cheerios cereal
- 5 cups Chex or Life cereal
- 2 cups peanuts
- 1 (14-ounce) bag plain M&Ms
- 1 (14-ounce) bag peanut M&Ms
- 2 cups mini marshmallows
- 2 (12-ounce) bags vanilla baking chips
- 3 tablespoons vegetable oil

1. Mix the pretzels, cereals, peanuts, M&Ms, and marshmallows together in an extra-large bowl or pot. If you don't have a big enough bowl, you can divide them between 2 bowls. Set aside.

2. Combine the vanilla chips and oil in a microwave-safe medium bowl. Melt in

CG! tip: Add your own personal twist to this recipe. Replace the M&Ms with Reese's Pieces, try caramel corn instead of peanuts, or use all of them. The best part of this snack is that pretty much anything goes. So have fun experimenting until you find your favorite combination of sweet and salty treats. Yum!

the microwave for 30 seconds. Stir and check to see if the texture is creamy enough to pour. If not, continue to heat and stir, 30 seconds at a time.

3. Slowly add the melted vanilla over the dry mixture and stir. Repeat until you've used all the vanilla and everything is evenly covered.

4. Spread the mixture in a waxed paper–lined pan. You may need more than one pan to fit the whole batch. Let cool until the vanilla coating has hardened, about 2 hours.

5. Break the snack up into small, manageable pieces and serve in a giant bowl with plastic cups for scooping and eating.

girly gumball fizz

For each drink, fill a glass a little less than ½ way with pink lemonade. Fill the remainder of the glass with Sprite or 7 UP, add a splash of lime juice, and stir. Throw in one or two gumballs and watch as the gum dissolves and the colored dye creates pretty swirls in the glass! Just make sure to tell guests to be careful not to swallow the gumballs while they are drinking.

bond girls

Valentine's Day may have started out as a gushy couples' holiday, but it's really a time to connect with anyone and everyone who's special to you, especially your best friends. Try one or more of these fun ideas that will help you share the love and bring you all closer than ever.

Show your heart. Celebrate the day of love with temporary heart tattoos. Help each other put them on in the same spot (like the inside of your wrists). Then when you're back at school, everyone will see the Valentine ties that you all share.

String each other along. Wrap a red string around one another's wrists and secure it with seven knots. Make a wish for your friendship with each knot you tie. Wear them as long as you can—that is, until they fall off on their own!

Light up your lives. Sit in a circle. Take turns lighting your own small yellow candle (yellow represents friendship) and sharing a story that shows how special each girl's friendship is. When everyone has had a turn, use the candles to light one large yellow one to symbolize your everlasting unity.

Make a soul sister scrapbook. Tell your friends to bring their favorite photos and items that remind them of special moments in your friendships (like ticket stubs or birthday cards). Glue them onto the pages of a scrapbook, then take turns being the keeper of the book. Next Valentine's, add a "new" chapter with another year of memories.

See her future. Sit in a circle with a lit candle in the center and all stare at it for ten minutes. As your vision gets hazy, focus your thoughts on the girl to your right (while still staring at the flame) and think about her future. Then go around and share the visions you each had with the group.

chick rock playlist

- "Big Girls Don't Cry," Fergie
- "All I Wanna Do," Sheryl Crow
- "Bitch," Meredith Brooks
- "Hollaback Girl," Gwen Stefani
- "Girls Just Want to Have Fun," Cyndi Lauper
- "Independent Woman," Destiny's Child
- "We Are Family," Sister Sledge

chick flick therapy

Need a cinematic lift? Whether V-day has you feeling up or down, screen a film that will fit your mood.

Get over him. Get your girls over their breakup blues with one of these heartbreak-healers:

- *Hope Floats*
- *The Man in the Moon*

Celebrate your bond. Go girl-power crazy with one of these classic tearjerkers:

- *Beaches*
- *Now and Then*
- *Steel Magnolias*

Get the giggles. Remember how silly and exciting love can be with one of these funny favorites:

- *Bridget Jones's Diary*
- *Never Been Kissed*
- *How to Lose a Guy in 10 Days*

HAPPY V-DAY!

oscar **night bash**

Roll out the red carpet for your movie-obsessed friends on Oscar Sunday, and the award for most glamorous hostess will go to *you*! $$$

glamour invites

The invitation should convey elegance: Use a gold marker on black cardstock with gold envelopes.

Include Oscar ballots with all the nominees in the top categories listed. Collect them at the start of the party, then give a prize to the guest who gets the most right.

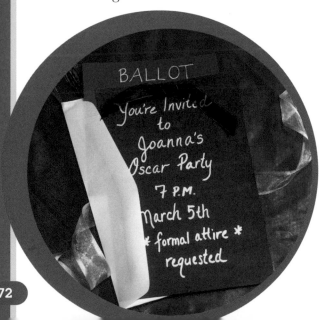

award-winning decorations

▪ Glam up a coffee table with orange satin and gold tulle.

▪ Tulips in plastic popcorn boxes make fun centerpieces.

▪ Lots of gold helium balloons will instantly glitz up a white wall.

▪ Add flair with a clapboard and a film reel to hold drinks.

red carpet playlist

▪ "Celebrity," *NSYNC

▪ "You're a Superstar," Love Inc.

▪ "Fame," Irene Cara

▪ "Superstar," Usher

▪ "Paparazzi," Switchfoot

DRINK!
celebrity spritzer

Mix all of the ingredients together in a large bowl and stir to combine. Ladle into fancy glasses and garnish each with 2 or 3 raspberries.

EAT!
paparazzi pizza

1. Preheat the oven to 400°F. Spray olive oil lightly on cookie sheets. Using a 2-inch round cookie cutter (at baking supply stores), cut out 30 mini tortillas from the large ones. Place on the cookie sheets, leaving an inch between each one.

2. Spread about 1 tablespoon tomato sauce on each tortilla. Sprinkle a little of each kind of cheese on top. Bake pizzas for 10 minutes, or until the cheese is melted and the tortillas are slightly crispy.

3. Serve with small bowls of chopped pepperoni, oregano, chili flakes, and salt and pepper so guests can top their pizzas as they like.

ROLL OUT THE RED CARPET!

oscar bingo

1. Create game cards on cardstock with four rows across and four columns down. Write things you're likely to see (or not!) at the show (e.g., actress in a red dress, actor crying during a speech) in each box. Mix up ideas on each card.

2. Give one card to each guest to check off as you watch. The first person to check off all in a row or a column wins!

CG! tip: To make celeb coasters: Cut photos of your favorite stars from magazines. Glue onto circles of cork, cut around the photo, then rest your drink on a nominee's face!

hollywood star favors

Take Polaroids of your guests as they arrive. Tape them on gold stars and give each one a funny award, like "Best Sick-Day Performance." Give to guests as souvenirs as they walk out the door.

😮 CG! ouch: tan-gerine!

❝ I am a pale-skinned person and I had never been self-conscious about it until I was invited to an older guy's party. I went out and bought some dark sunless tanner because I wanted to look tan and sexy for the party. So when I was getting ready I put three layers on each leg, not knowing it gets darker as it dries. I showed up with orange legs but I was sand pale everywhere else! Everyone made fun of me. I felt so dumb!"

fall for **autumn dinner** party

School starting to get to you? Well, give yourself (and all your good friends!) something to look forward to—a dinner party! It's a time for everyone to relax, reconnect, and remember that you're all in this life thing together. **$$$**

autumn invites

Cut out squares and rectangles from autumn-colored origami paper (at art supply stores). With a silver paint pen (at art supply stores), write the party info in sections on each piece. Put the pieces in a colored envelope—guests will have to spill out the "leaves" and arrange them to get the scoop! Be personal—hand out invites in person.

cosmogirl! cornucopia

Remember back in the third grade you learned how the Pilgrims celebrated their abundant harvest with a horn of plenty? Well, here's our version. Start with a basket lined with cornhusks and filled with popcorn. Place a mix of nuts, raisins, fruits, and other festive foods around it on the table for an "undone" cornucopia (minus the horn!). Then tell everyone to nibble the centerpiece!

3-2-1 **party!**

table-setting how-tos

■ Arrange silk leaves (at craft stores) loosely under plates as place mats.

■ Make napkins from old dresses or sheets (or try the discount bin at a fabric store). Cut fabric into squares and tie with strips of cornhusks, ribbon, whatever!

PLAY!

truth or lie?

Place a slip of paper under each plate. Leave pens on the table. Have each guest write down her name, plus two obscure facts about herself (like "I used to eat bugs!") and one lie (that she makes up) and write "lie" next to it. Put all of the slips of paper into a bowl. Then have someone read each person's name and their two truths and lie. Ask everyone to guess which statements are facts—and which one isn't!

EAT!

pretzels and dip

INGREDIENTS
- 1 jar hot fudge sauce
- 1 bottle honey mustard
- 1 package walnut raisin cream cheese
- 3 large bags of pretzel rods, twists, and nuggets
MAKES 6 SERVINGS.

Scoop the fudge, mustard, and cream cheese into separate dishes. Serve on a large tray with each type of pretzel neatly arranged around the different dips.

DRINK!

italian sodas

For each drink, fill an 8-ounce glass halfway with crushed ice. Add 2 ounces Italian syrup (get a few flavors in the coffee aisle at the grocery stores) and a little more than 5 ounces plain seltzer. Garnish with a pretty swizzle stick and serve!

buffalo roasted chicken

individually mixed ice cream

INGREDIENTS
- olive oil spray
- 2 eggs
- 1 cup breadcrumbs
- 1 tablespoon chili powder
- 1 teaspoon salt
- 1/2 teaspoon cayenne pepper
- 6 boneless, skinless chicken breasts
- 1 (8-ounce) container sour cream
- 4 ounces blue cheese, crumbled
- 3 celery stalks

MAKES 6 SERVINGS.

INGREDIENTS
- 2 (1/2 gallon) cartons ice cream (1 vanilla, 1 chocolate—or other flavors if you like)
- toppings: sprinkles, candy, nuts, cookie pieces, etc.
- mini candy canes
- fresh mint leaves

MAKES 14 TO 16 SERVINGS.

1. Preheat the oven to 400°F. Lightly spray a large baking pan with olive oil spray and set aside.

2. Beat the eggs in a shallow bowl. In a separate shallow bowl, mix the bread-crumbs, chili powder, salt, and cayenne pepper. One at a time, dip the chicken pieces into the egg, then into the breadcrumb mixture to coate evenly. Place on the baking sheet.

3. Bake for about 20 minutes. Cut into the center of one. The juices should be clear, and the meat should not be pink. If they're not done, keep baking in 5-minute intervals, testing until done.

4. For the dip, mix the sour cream and blue cheese in a small bowl. Cut the celery into 1/2x3-inch sticks. Serve the chicken on a platter with the celery and dip on the side.

1. Remove the cartons from both the blocks of ice cream, placing the ice cream on pre-chilled chop-ping boards. Slice off a portion of ice cream (like you would a cake) using a spatula; leave it on the chopping board.

2. Ask a guest to pick toppings. Take a teaspoon of each of her choices. Use the spatula to crush and completely mix all of the toppings into the ice cream. Place in a small bowl. Garnish with a candy cane and a mint leaf.

3. Repeat until you've created a custom-ized bowl of ice cream for each of your guests. Then make yours and enjoy!

3-2-1 party!

super bowl **party**

You'll score major points when you invite friends over to chill out and watch the big game. Whip up some couch potato–friendly finger foods and start your party victory dance! $$$

gridiron invites

SUPPLIES
- football-themed, printer-friendly blank invitations and matching envelopes
- multicolored star confetti
- markers

1. Type up your party info on a computer and print out on the blank invitations; or you can just neatly hand-write the info on it with the markers.

2. Place the invitations in the matching envelopes. Place a bunch of star confetti in each envelope so that it spills out when opened. Mail or hand out to friends at school.

get that "go team!" spirit

Tell guests to come wearing their team's colors.

Use cups, plates, and napkins in team colors.

Fill bowls with whistles and mini toy footballs to play with during halftime and commercials.

You're invited to Meredith's Annual

All-Star Football Party
Jets vs. Broncos
Sunday, November 20th
4:00 p.m.
3434 Ridge Road
RSVP to Meredith
Wear Your Team Colors!

EAT!
perfect pigskin menu

Pregame snack: Warm Spinach Dip

Halftime treat: Frozen pizza

Game noshes: Bags of popcorn and bowls of M&Ms in team colors

Drinks: Sideline Coolers

Postgame sweets: Customized Cupcakes

DRINK!
sideline coolers

INGREDIENTS
- 3 cups crushed ice
- 1 quart iced tea
- 1 quart lemonade
- 1 lemon, cut into slices

MAKES 10 SERVINGS.

Fill an oversized punch bowl with the crushed ice. Combine the iced tea and lemonade in it and mix well. Garnish with the lemon slices and add a ladle for serving.

EAT!
warm spinach dip

INGREDIENTS
- 2 (9-ounce) packages frozen creamed spinach, thawed
- 3 2/3 cups shredded Swiss cheese
- 1 tablespoon pepper
- 1/2 teaspoon salt
- 1 large round loaf sourdough bread
- pretzels

1. Preheat the oven to 350°F. Mix the spinach, cheese, pepper, and salt, in a large bowl. Cut the top off the bread. Carefully remove the soft bread inside, leaving a 1-inch-thick bowl. Cut the inside of bread into bite-sized pieces and set aside. Pour the spinach dip into the bowl.

2. Wrap the bread bowl in foil but leave the dip exposed. Bake for 45 minutes, or until the dip is warm (carefully taste to test). Serve with pretzels and the bread pieces for dipping.

TOUCHDOWN!

3-2-1 party!

customized cupcakes

INGREDIENTS

- 1 cup (2 sticks) unsalted butter, softened
- 2 cups sugar
- 4 large eggs, at room temperature
- 1 1/2 cups self-rising flour
- 1 1/4 cups all-purpose flour
- 1 cup milk
- 1 teaspoon vanilla extract
- 2 (16-ounce) tubs chocolate and vanilla frosting
- toppings: candy, sprinkles, chocolate chips, etc.

MAKES 24 CUPCAKES.

1. Preheat the oven to 350°F. Line two 12-cup muffin tins with paper cupcake liners. In a large bowl, using an electric mixer on medium speed, cream the butter until smooth. Add the sugar gradually and beat until fluffy, about 3 minutes.

2. Add the eggs and beat well. Slowly add both kinds of flour, the milk, and vanilla extract, beating well between each addition.

3. Spoon the batter into the cups, filling them about three-fourths full. Bake 20 minutes, or until the tops spring back when touched. Cool completely.

4. Set up a toppings bar with frosting in the teams' colors, all the toppings and let guests ice and decorate their own cupcakes!

football favors

Buy plastic footballs with candy whistles ($11 for 9) at blaircandy.com. Open each football and add a few pieces of candy or chocolate, along with the candy whistles. Close, place them all in a basket, and display as decoration during the party. Then hand them out to guests as they leave.

secret santa
holiday party

Want to give the best present ever? Then throw a party that'll bring joy to little kids in need. **$$**

secret santa 101

You know Santa doesn't come down your chimney, but you'll probably *still* wake up to tons of presents. For millions of children in need, though, the holidays come and go without any gifts. Now you can answer children's letters to Santa (the post office collects them!) and help make dreams come true by sending them beautifully wrapped presents (and cards). So gather your friends for a marathon "wrap" party—and get ready to play the jolly guy himself! This season, you'll get the greatest gift of all—a warm fuzzy!

party countdown

You'd better make this list and check it twice to stay organized!

A month before the party: Go to the post office to pick up letters to Santa (take just one for each guest).

Three weeks before: Send an Evite (evite.com) with the party info: day, time, place, and your reason for throwing it. Schedule it for no later than December 15 so the gifts will arrive by Christmas. When a guest RSVPs yes, give or send her a kid's letter.

One or two weeks before: Select a letter and shop for your child's present. (Be creative. You can get a great gift for under $25.) Gather wrapping supplies.

Day before: Cut out and bake cookies, but don't decorate.

BE A SECRET SANTA!

festive santa's workshop

■ Be sure to have lots of tabletop space and plenty of wrapping paper and decorating supplies so everyone can create super gifts.

■ Ask everyone to bring her favorite holiday CD to play while you're wrapping.

■ Have each person read her child's letter out loud to share their stories.

■ Play a holiday video like *How the Grinch Stole Christmas* on mute in the background as a festive but easy "decoration."

■ After wrapping, reward all your elves with DIY Christmas cookies. Before the party, cut out shapes from a roll of sugar-cookie dough, then bake. Guests can frost, decorate, and eat them after you've finished the gifts.

cards from santa

SUPPLIES
- construction paper
- green and white felt
- scissors
- glue
- rhinestones
- metallic paper
- acrylic paint
- 1-inch-wide ribbons

Make one-of-a-kind cards to accompany your special gifts.

Fold construction paper in half to form cards. Then try one or all of these ideas:

Tree card: Cut a tree from felt and glue it to the card. Glue on rhinestones. Cut "presents" from metallic paper and glue under the tree.

Stocking card: Cut a stocking shape out of paper in a contrasting color to the card. Glue it on. Cut child's name

out of metallic paper. Glue letters on stocking. Cut a felt rectangle; glue along the top of the stocking.

Bow card: Lay cards on top of newspaper. Splatter red and silver paint on the cards, then let dry for an hour. Wrap ribbons around the cards and tie a bow to close.

Make sure to write a cute note inside and sign your card "Love, Santa."

customized gift wrap

Wrap gifts in various solid or graphic print papers, or dress up brown bags to save money. Decorate with the basic supplies used for the cards (with some additional items). Try these ideas:

Weave: Cut strips of green ribbon. Wrap them around the present lengthwise, evenly spaced. Tape ribbon down with double-stick tape. Repeat crosswise with red ribbon, weaving it over and under green.

Tree: Make a felt tree to match the one on the card. Cut a squiggly piece of green felt for grass. Glue them onto a wrapped gift.

Bow: On each end of a piece of ribbon (first measure length to fit box), write child's name in puff paint. Tie ribbon around the present.

post-party wrap-up

Help your mom load up the car to take all the presents to the post office at once. Remember: Don't use *your* return address or name! Write "Santa Claus, North Pole."

BE A SECRET SANTA!

earth day **swap party**

Recycle, reuse, and reap the benefits when you throw a clothes-swapping soiree. $$$

SET THE MOOD!
earth-friendly invites

Raid a thrift store—or your closet—for cute vintage tees. Get the eco vibe going by writing info (including a request to bring swap-worthy duds)on big green leaves (a paint pen should work). Punch a hole in the leaf and tie it to a shirt's tag with string. Your friends can keep their tees or swap them at the party!

SET THE MOOD!
earth day décor

- Pick a springy color theme, like green and lavender.
- Bright throw rugs are comfy to sit on while swapping.
- Serve sandwiches and salad on recycled plastic plates and utensils.

SET THE MOOD!
bag centerpieces

Take a leftover shopping bag and cut down about 3 inches just outside the handles, then cut around the sides so the top of the bag has two flaps. Tape the flaps together to create a new, wide handle. Fill with fresh flowers.

GUESS
BY MARCIANO

PLAY!
shop 'n' swap!

Ask friends to bring a few clothing items in good condition that they are willing to swap for other girls' clothes. String up a clothing line to easily display the stuff. After your swap, donate any leftover clothes to charity.

GREEN PARTY!

EAT!
roasted veggie sandwiches

SERVE LUNCH BEFORE THE SHOP 'N' SWAP SO YOU DON'T GET FOOD ON THE CLOTHES!

INGREDIENTS

- 1 organic yellow squash
- 1 organic eggplant
- 1 organic red bell pepper
- 1 organic yellow bell pepper
- 1 organic onion, peeled
- sea salt
- ground pepper
- 1/4 cup olive oil
- 5 Portuguese rolls
- 1 (8-ounce) tub hummus
- 1 (8-ounce) package feta cheese
- fresh bean sprouts

MAKES 5 SERVINGS.

DRINK!
watermelon slushy

USE THE WATERMELON RIND AS

- 1 large organic seedless watermelon
- 3 cups pomegranate juice
- Organic liquid cane sugar, to taste

MAKES ABOUT 8 SERVINGS.

1. Preheat the oven to 400°F. Slice the vegetables lengthwise into thin strips. Toss in a big bowl with the olive oil, salt, and pepper. Spread out in single layers on baking sheets. Roast about 10 minutes, or until soft. Or brown them on a grill for 4 to 7 minutes on each side.

2. Slice the rolls open; scoop out some of the bread. Spread a thick layer of hummus on each side of the rolls. Put on a layer of veggies, sprinkle on cheese and sprouts, and add another layer of veggies. Finish with a bit more cheese and close the sandwiches!

A BOWL FOR THE SLUSHY. FUN!

Cut the melon in half lengthwise. Scoop out the pulp and place in thin single layers on foil-lined baking sheets. Put in freezer for 3 hours, or until frozen. Blend the frozen chunks and pomegranate juice in a blender on high until slushy. Stir in the liquid sugar. Serve in one hollowed-out half of the melon rind.

■ Add a pre-packaged mixed organic green salad to your lunch.

fiesta **fever**

Head south—of the border, that is—and throw this Mexican fiesta that will have you shaking your maracas. *¡Ay caramba!* $$$

SET THE MOOD!
south-of-the-border invites

YOUR PARTY'S GOING TO BE A SCORCHER! TURN UP THE HEAT WITH MINI TABASCO BOTTLES FOR EACH OF YOUR GUESTS.

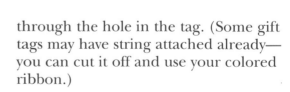

SUPPLIES
- Mini Tabasco bottles
- Paper gift tags
- red and green markers
- thin red, green, and white ribbon
- scissors

1. Write the party details out in marker on the gift tags. Cut a piece of ribbon about 6 inches long. Thread ribbon through the hole in the tag. (Some gift tags may have string attached already—you can cut it off and use your colored ribbon.)

2. Double knot the ribbon around the neck of each Tabasco bottle to firmly attach each gift tag. Hand out to your guests.

go mexican wild!

■ Cover the table with a bright colored tablecloth. Place a large sombrero in the middle and fill with colorful flowers (remove stems first). Try Gerbera daisies—they come in eye popping bright colors and are inexpensive too.

■ Little potted baby cacti make great decorations—scatter them around the table and other parts of the room. Bonus: They also make great favors! Send each guest home with one at the end of the night.

■ Frida Kahlo was a famous Mexican artist who made wild colorful paintings. Hang up a bunch of her posters or find a book of her art and use a color copier to blow up your favorite images. "Frame" the art with bright crepe paper or garlands.

■ String up some chili pepper lights, dim the overheads, and get ready to fiesta.

crazy cascorones!

CASCORONES ARE LIKE A CROSS BETWEEN A PIÑATA AND AN EASTER EGG. MEXICAN TRADITION SAYS HAVING ONE BROKEN (GENTLY!) OVER YOUR HEAD WILL BRING YOU GOOD LUCK.

SUPPLIES
- scissors
- 1 dozen large eggs
- confetti
- tissue paper
- rubber cement

1. Using the point of the scissors, carefully punch a quarter size hole in the bottom (the wider) end of an egg. Go slowly so you don't crack the whole shell. Drain the egg over the sink (or into a bowl, and make huevos rancheros for dinner!). Rinse out the empty shell. Repeat with the remaining eggs and let dry overnight.

2. Fill the shell half way with confetti. Use a thin layer of glue and cover the hole with a small piece of tissue paper. You can glue over just the hole or wrap the entire egg in paper. Let the *cascarones* dry overnight.

3. Place them all in a basket and invite guests to get cracking!

sparkling non-alcoholic sangria

INGREDIENTS

- 1 orange with peel, cut into wedges
- 1 lemon with peel, cut into wedges
- 1 lime with peel, cut into wedges
- 1 small apple, cut into wedges
- 4 cups red grape juice
- 3 cups sparkling cider
- 1 cup orange juice or lemonade
- sugar to taste

1. Pour the grape juice into a large pitcher. Squeeze the juice from the orange, lemon, and lime wedges into the grape juice and stir. Toss in the wedges. Toss in the apple pieces. (You'll probably want to use only half of the fruit since it will be a lot when it's cut up.) Place the pitcher in the fridge for up to four hours so the fruit can soak and get soft.

2. Add a teaspoon of sugar, the orange juice or lemonade, and the sparkling cider and stir. Taste and add more sugar if you want. Place the pitcher in the fridge and chill until serving.

seven-layer nachos

NOBODY CAN RESIST A PLATE OF NACHOS!

INGREDIENTS

- 1 1/2 cups sour cream
- 1 package taco seasoning mix
- 2 (16-ounce) jars bean dip
- 2 (8-ounce) containers guacamole
- 1 bunch green onions, chopped
- 1 (14.5-ounce) can diced tomatoes
- 1 (8-ounce) can black olives
- 1 (8-ounce) package shredded Cheddar cheese
- 1 (8-ounce) package shredded Monterey Jack cheese
- tortilla chips

MAKES 8-10 SERVINGS.

1. Mix together the sour cream and taco seasoning in a small bowl—add the seasoning a little at a time, stir, and taste until it's spicy enough for you.

2. On a large round platter start layering the ingredients as follows: Place the bean dip as the first layer on the outer edge of the platter, then add the guacamole, followed by the sour cream mixture, green onions, tomatoes, black olives, and then the cheeses. The layers will get smaller as you get closer to the center of your "circle." You can fill the whole platter or leave an opening in the center to add tortilla chips. Serve with a larger basket of additional chips for dipping.

EAT!
dunking donuts

CHURROS, FRIED DOUGH SPRINKLED WITH CINNAMON AND SUGAR AND DIPPED IN CREAMY CHOCOLATE, ARE A MEXICAN FAVORITE. TRY THIS EASY AND QUICK INTERPRETATION.

INGREDIENTS
- 1 box cinnamon donut holes
- 1 jar hot fudge or chocolate syrup
- cinnamon sugar spice
  MAKES 8-10 SERVINGS.

1. Place a toothpick in each donut hole and arrange them on a tray. (Check a party store for red and green frilled cocktail picks or even ones with Mexican flags.)

2. Transfer the hot fudge or chocolate syrup to a bowl and heat in the microwave for a few seconds at a time until warm. Spoon cinnamon sugar in another small bowl and serve with the donuts for dipping.

PLAY!
kiss the pig
SPICE THINGS UP BY ORGANIZING A GAME FOR YOUR GUESTS.

1. Sit with your friends in a circle (alternating boy-girl) and pass around an imaginary pig, clockwise.

2. Ask each player to name and kiss a different part of the "pig" when they get it. (And keep it clean, Senorita! Dirty minds get disqualified!)

3. After the pig makes it around once, tell everyone to kiss the player to their left—on the same spot where they kissed the pig! *Olé!*

red hot beats

- ◼ "Livin' la Vida Loca," Ricky Martin
- ◼ "Let's Get Loud," Jennifer Lopez
- ◼ "It's Gettin' Hot in Here," Nelly
- ◼ "I Need to Know," Marc Anthony
- ◼ "Spice Up Your Life," Spice Girls
- ◼ "Bailamos," Enrique Iglesias
- ◼ "Hot Hot Hot," Buster Poindexter

spa-tacular **pre-prom party**

Gossip with your girls and figure out how you'll spend all the money you're saving on salon treatments. Hum-V limo anyone?!

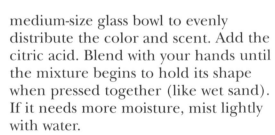

SET THE MOOD!
fizzy bath bombs invites

SUPPLIES

- 1 1/2 cups baking soda
- 1/2 teaspoon water-based food coloring
- 1/2 teaspoon fragrance oil of your choice
- 3/4 cup citric acid (find it at natural food stores)
- water in a spray bottle, if needed
- 1 ball-shape soap or candy mold (2 1/2-inch diameter)
- wax paper
- cookie sheet
- cellophane gift wrap
- colorful narrow ribbon
- paper tags
- markers

1. Mix together the baking soda, food coloring, and fragrance oil in a medium-size glass bowl to evenly distribute the color and scent. Add the citric acid. Blend with your hands until the mixture begins to hold its shape when pressed together (like wet sand). If it needs more moisture, mist lightly with water.

2. Pack some of the mixture tightly into each half of the mold. Level off and wipe away any excess. Gently press out each half onto a waxed paper–lined cookie sheet. Repeat with the remaining baking soda mixture. Refrigerate the mixture overnight.

3. The next day, remove the bath bombs from the fridge. Gently place two halves together to form a sphere.

4. Wrap in cellophane and tie each end with ribbon. Write the party info on a paper tag. (Remember to ask guests to bring a bathrobe, flip flops, and any beauty supplies they want.) Thread a tag on to one of the ribbons holding the cellophane closed. Knot the end so it stays in place. Hand the bombs out to your guests and get ready for an explosive reaction!

CG! tip: Too busy with last minute prom prep to DIY? Buy small soaps or scented votive candles from the dollar store or drug store, wrap them in cellophane, tie with ribbons, and attach the party details.

OH SO PRETTY!

spa guide

Turn your house into a four-star spa with these ahh-inspiring ideas.

Set a tranquil scene. Close the shades, dim the lights, and light plenty of scented candles (just don't leave them burning unattended!). Download a bunch of soft, new age music to play while you're primping.

Welcome guests into a stress-free zone. Greet your friends at the door and ask them to leave their cell phones, iPods, and PDAs in a designated area— away from where the spa action will take place. Leave a pile of neatly folded, fluffy towels in the entryway and lead guests to a bathroom where they can change into their bathrobe and flip flops.

Gather your supplies. Set aside one area for all your beauty ammo. Fill glass jars and little baskets with cotton balls, Q-tips, nail files, polish, and other necessities. Raid a dollar store for cute pump-style containers and spray bottles, then fill them with hand lotions, polish remover, face creams, and face masks. Make sure to label them so you don't get mixed up.

3-2-1 **party!**

Create manicure stations. Drape several snack tables in soft, pretty fabrics and arrange them around the room with two chairs (one on either side of each table) so your friends can work on each other's nails. Leave a bowl of hot soapy water at each station for soaking. Place a large fan (or several small ones if you have) nearby so guests can take turns sitting in front of it to dry their nails.

PLAY!

manicure moves

Get a salon-style manicure in five easy steps. Share them with your friends—then go give each other a hand!

1. Shape your nails with the rough filing side of a filer-buffer tool so they're square with rounded edges and 1/4-inch long tips. Smooth any ridges with the fine buffing sides.

2. Mix 1 tablespoon olive oil and 2/3 cup warm water in a bowl. Soak nails in it for 3 minutes to soften cuticles. Afterward, push them back with an orange stick.

CG! special touch

Impress your guests with a soy massage candle. Lots of companies are making these cool candles that double as skin care (search for them online). Light one for 20 minutes, until wax pools in the center. Blow out the flame, wait a few moments to let it cool, then dip your fingers into the wax and massage into your cuticles or hands.

3. Massage hand cream (or candle wax—see "special touch") into your hands in circular motions, from cuticles to wrists. Then clean nails off with polish remover—polish lasts longer on clean, dry nails.

4. Apply a clear base coat, then paint on two coats of color from nail base to tip. Let dry for 10 minutes. Follow with clear topcoat to prevent chipping and add shine.

5. Let your nails dry for a full 15 minutes before touching them.

pedicure pointers

Play footsie with your friends and help each other get prom-ready piggies.

1. Use toenail clippers to trim all your toenails straight across. Leave at least 1/8-inch of white nail showing at the tips so you don't get ingrowns. Ow!

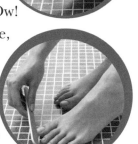

2. With a long nail file, smooth away the sharp edges along the tips of your toenail, then round off the corners slightly, the same way you do for fingernails.

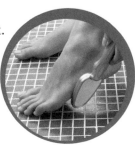

3. Rub hand or foot cream onto your feet. Then exfoliate any rough patches with a foot file. Rinse and towel-dry, then clean your toenails with polish remover.

4. Stroke a base coat onto toenails, then apply two coats of polish. Seal your handiwork with a topcoat.

5. Kick back for at least 15 minutes while toes dry.

> ! **CG! party lines**
> " For my 13th birthday party, I threw a spa party which I liked to call a sparty! There was this cool company that came to my house and set up a mani/pedi station, a massage station, and a facial station. It was all professionally done, all in my very own basement! It was the perfect girls night, complete with my favorite movie of all time, *13 Going On 30*. It was absolutely fab-u-lous!"
>
> —Kelly, Centreville, VA

EAT!

spa snacks

Wet nails and goopy face masks will make it hard to eat. So keep things light and easy. These quick and healthy choices will keep your energy up and your stress-level down.

- Hummus and pita breads
- Cheese and fruit platter
- Fruit flavored smoothies
- Veggies and dip (try our yummy cucumber recipe)
- Air-popped popcorn mixed with raisins and almonds

EAT!

cool as a cucumber yogurt dip

WHIP UP THIS LIGHT AND CREAMY DIP AND MAKE SURE TO SAVE SOME CUCUMBER SLICES FOR YOUR FACIAL— PLACE THEM ON YOUR LIDS TO REDUCE ANY EYE PUFFIES!

CG! tip: Banish pre-prom bloating— skip the carbonated drinks! Instead, take a cue from real spas and set out a large pitcher of ice water with lemon slices on a fancy tray so guests can sip while they de-stress.

INGREDIENTS

- 2 medium cucumbers
- 4 teaspoons salt
- 2 cups plain nonfat yogurt
- 4 cloves garlic, minced
- 1 tablespoon chopped fresh mint
- 1 tablespoon chopped fresh dill
- 4 teaspoons lemon juice
- 6 whole wheat pitas
- assorted sliced veggies

1. Peel the cucumbers, then slice lengthwise, scoop out the seeds, and discard. Grate with a cheese grater. Put the grated cucumbers in a clean paper towel and squeeze out as much moisture as you can over the sink. Place in a bowl and mix in the salt. Refrigerate for 1 hour.

2. Remove the cucumbers from the fridge and stir in the yogurt, garlic, mint, dill, and lemon juice. Refrigerate for 2 hours. Serve the dip with pita triangles and sliced veggies.

TAKE AWAY!

happy zen-ding!

Give your guests the ultimate take-away goody: a sense of serenity. Finish the day with a quiet meditation. Leave the lights dim and the music on low and have everyone sit cross-legged on the floor with their eyes closed. Spend 5 or 10 minutes sitting in the stillness, breathing deeply and focusing on the music or envisioning the amazing night you're about to have.

OH SO PRETTY

star-spangled **soiree**

Throw a Fourth of July bash in a few easy steps— use the extra time to buy a sizzling new outfit! $$

SET THE MOOD!
star spangled décor

■ Set the scene by draping 5 to 6 yards of sheer red and white fabric horizontally across two trees, letting it flow down over the branches. Set up several snack tables underneath and cover them in the same material.

■ Don't just wish upon the stars when you can kiss upon them too! Hang silver cardboard stars from the trees. Mark some with a bright red lip print— if guests get caught under those stars, then it's smooching time for them!

PLAY!
wading game

Cool off your guests on a hot summer night by setting up kiddie pools in the yard. Add water and wade away! For mood lighting, float red, white, and blue star candles in them.

RED, HOT, AND BLUE!

EAT!
mini bbq

Cut burgers (including buns!) into bite-sized pieces and heat up a bunch of cocktail pigs-in-blanket (figure on 4 or 5 mini burgers and 6 to 8 mini dogs per guest). Don't forget some veggie burgers, too! Serve with ketchup and mustard, and lots of napkins!

DRINK!
slush puppies

INGREDIENTS
- 6 tablespoons sugar
- 4 to 5 cups ice cubes
- 1 cup prepared red Kool-Aid
- 1 cup lemonade
- 1 cup blue Gatorade

MAKES ABOUT 3 SERVINGS.

1. Using the pulse setting on a blender, combine 2 tablespoons of the sugar with 1 cup of ice cubes and the Kool-Aid. Add more ice cubes, a few at a time, and blend until the mixture is slushy. Fill 3 tall glasses one-third with the red slush.

2. Repeat the process with the lemonade and then again with the Gatorade. You will create layered red, white, and blue slushes in the glasses. Garnish with a mini American flag and serve.

EAT!
american pie

THIS SWEET "PIZZA" PIE IS SURE TO BE A HIT!

INGREDIENTS
- 4 (6-inch) frozen pizza crusts
- 6 teaspoons granulated sugar
- 1 pint strawberries, stems removed, halved
- 1 pint blueberries
- 1 teaspoon vanilla extract
- 1 1/2 cups whipped topping

MAKES 16 SERVINGS.

1. Defrost the crusts. Preheat the oven to 450°F. Place the crusts on baking sheets and sprinkle all over with 4 teaspoons of the sugar. Bake for 6 to 8 minutes, or until lightly golden. Cool for 5 minutes.

2. Combine the strawberries, blueberries, remaining 2 teaspoons sugar, and the vanilla extract in a large bowl. Cover each crust evenly with a thin layer of whipped cream, then spread the fruit topping over the cream. Cut each pie into four slices and serve.

v.i.p. **pool party**

Break out the velvet rope. This exclusive poolside soiree will be the talk of the town and everyone's going to want a ticket in. **$$**

SET THE MOOD!
flip flop fandango

Buy several pairs of cheap flip flops in a variety of colors and sizes (try a dollar store or some craft stores). Write the party info in marker on the bottom of every flip flop (each guest will get just one, not the whole pair) or write out on notecards and attach to flip flops with ribbon. Tell guests to bring the sandal to the party and then get them mingling by searching for their sole-mate!

POSH
POOLSIDE
SPLASH

SET THE MOOD!
pool party panache

■ Pick a sexy summery color theme like shiny metallics and crisp white and push it to the max. Incorporate white and shine wherever possible and ask guests to dress to match the theme too.

■ Use the pool as your centerpiece. Fill it with metallic silver, gold, and white balloons and then float large white lotus flowers (silk or fresh will both work). But reassure guests that the pool is *not* off limits. Everyone in for an evening dip!

■ String up white Christmas lights— wrap them around the deck, in a few trees, or around the entryway to the house. If you have some trees that are close together, create a makeshift cabana by draping long white sheer panels of fabric across several limbs.

3-2-1 **party!**

■ Plastic or paper dishes and silverware are more outdoor-friendly. Stock up on non-breakable tableware at the party store.

■ Consider ordering monogrammed cocktail napkins. You can get them made for as little as $23 for 100 (search online). They're a small little touch that will make a huge, sophisticated statement.

■ Keep bottled water and cans of soda on ice in big silver buckets or galvanized tins.

SET THE MOOD!

paper bag lanterns

CREATE A SEXY GLOW WITH THESE FESTIVE LUMINARIES.

SUPPLIES

- paper lunch bags (at supermarkets, or try craft stores for assorted colors)
- spray paint, optional
- stencil—try to pick something with simple lines and avoid anything too tiny—2x3 inches or larger is easiest to work with. Some ideas: stars, a sun and moon, your initials in block letters, or a butterfly)
- pencil
- scissors
- sand, rocks, or dirt (to weigh down the bags)
- tea lights or votive candles
- small glass votive holders

1. If you can't find colored paper bags and don't want to use plain brown ones, you can spray paint them. Lay them flat on newspaper (work outside or in a very well-ventilated area that you can get dirty) and spray paint the front and back completely. Then open the bag up and spray paint the 2 sides. Let dry 2 hours.

2. Lay one bag flat on a hard surface like the kitchen table. Take the stencil and place it down on the paper bag wherever you'd like. Trace the stencil shape onto the paper bag with a pencil. Make sure to hold the stencil down as you work so it doesn't slide around. Repeat on the other side of the bag. Cut around the lines you traced to create openings in the bag in the shape of your stencil. Repeat with as many bags as you'd like.

3. Fill each bag with a few handfuls of sand, rocks, or dirt to weigh it down. Place the bags around your pool, deck, and/or patio. Place a tea light or candle in a small glass votive holder and put the holder in a bag, twisting it down into the sand. Light each candle, then step back and check out the cool jack-o'lantern glow. (Don't leave lanterns unattended at any time.)

EAT!
it's a wrap

THINK OF THESE COOL HORS D'OEUVRES
AS TINY CHICKEN CAESAR SALADS!

INGREDIENTS

- 1 bag pre-washed Romaine lettuce
- 1 bottle Caesar salad dressing
- 1 (10 ounce) package precooked carved grilled chicken breasts
- grated Parmesan cheese
- 1 package croutons

MAKES 10-12 SERVINGS.

1. Rinse the lettuce and pat dry with a paper towel. Take a lettuce leaf and lay it flat. Place a small drop of Caesar dressing in the center. Arrange one or two small strips of chicken on top. Sprinkle with some Parmesan cheese.

2. Carefully spear a crouton with a toothpick. Neatly roll the lettuce leaf up to form a mini wrap and place the toothpick all the way through it to hold it together. Repeat to make more mini wraps. Serve with a bowl of Caesar dressing for dipping.

EAT!
small wonders

Nothing screams chic party like cool, bite-sized appetizers that are circulated on shiny trays. Recruit your big bro to play waiter for the evening and promise him all the leftovers! Try some of these appetizing ideas:

- sushi rolls
- waffle fries (stock up at your favorite fast food joint, then divide into paper cones with toothpicks for easy eating)
- mini hamburgers (use a cookie cutter to cut out small portions from bigger burgers and buns)
- steamed dumplings (order from your local Chinese restaurant—we won't tell!)
- individual servings of mac 'n' cheese in mini take-out containers

POSH POOLSIDE SPLASH

DRINK!
mint metropolitan mocktails

For each mocktail, wet the rim of a glass. Pour some sugar into a small plate. Dip the rim of the glass into the sugar to coat the top. Place 3-4 fresh mint leaves at the bottom of the glass and crush with a wooden spoon. Add 1¼ teaspoons of lime juice (fresh or bottled) and 2 teaspoons sugar and mix together with the mint. Fill the glass a quarter of the way with crushed ice. Pour lime-flavored seltzer over the ice. Stir well. Garnish with a wedge of lime and a swizzle stick.

EAT!
sweet surprise

Ice cream sandwiches go chic when you use unexpected cookie/ice cream combinations. Try a scoop of mint chocolate chip between 2 Mallomars, pair raspberry sorbet and graham crackers or mocha chip with Nilla wafers. Serve these babies up as an *après*-swim treat—they're sure to make a big splash!

TAKE AWAY!
glam gift bags

Celebrity shindigs always end with a to-die-for gift bag—but you don't have to spend a mint because everyone loves free stuff, no matter how big or small! Fill white or metallic mini shopping bags with a variety of fun gifts like candy, bottled water, mini inflatable beach balls, or other novelty items (to save cash, consider buying in bulk).

CG! tip: Arrange the gift bags on a table near the festivities so they look great with the décor and entice your guests as they walk past them all night.

dog day **afternoon**

Don't make your pup beg! Show her some love and throw this backyard bash that will satisfy all your party animals. $$

paw print invites

> **SUPPLIES**
> - scissors
> - cardstock (this is a bit heavier then regular paper; it comes in a variety of colors and sizes at art supply stores or stationery stores)
> - markers
> - nontoxic children's finger paint
> - hole punch
> - ball-chain

1. Cut the cardstock into 4x10-inch rectangles. Write or print out the party details on the cards. Don't forget to invite guests and their dogs—or if they don't have one, maybe they can adopt a neighbor's dog for the day.

2. Gently dip your pup's paw into the finger paint and press it down on each invitation to leave behind a print. Be creative—have her "sign" her name at the bottom, or decorate the back of the card in multi-colored paw prints. (Make sure to wash your pup's paws thoroughly when you're done so she doesn't track paint all over the house.)

3. Punch a hole in the top corner of each card and thread a length of ball-chain through it to create a dog tag. Hand the tags out to your guests.

3-2-1 **party!**

101

SET THE MOOD!
pooch-proof your yard

Add these special touches to make your furry new friends feel at home.

Four-legged lounge: Create a VIP (very important pooch) area in one (preferably shady) part of the yard. Scatter dog beds, large throw pillows, and old blankets around for dogs to relax on. Leave out balls, stuffed animals, and other toys for them to play with.

Designer H20 bar: Line up several vinyl placemats on the grass or patio and put out several bowls of water. Check your local pet store for doggie vitamin water and even meat or chicken flavored water so all your guests have some beverage choices!

Wet 'n' wild: Fill up a kiddie pool with some water so the dogs can play and cool off. No pool? Turn on a sprinkler. Humans can take a run through too!

petiquette 101

■ Keep the party outside in a fenced in or well contained area. You don't want your house going to the dogs!

■ Consider limiting the number of guests for this event. Even though you'll be outdoors and there's lots of room, it could get tricky with too many energetic furballs running around!

■ Double check with guests that their dogs are all healthy and up-to-date on their shots.

■ Be prepared for accidents— keep plastic bags, paper towels, and disinfectant wipes on hand to clean up any messes.

grrr...eat games

Red Rover, Red Rover (of course!): The dogs will love running back and forth with you as you try to break through the other team's line.

Musical Mutts: Play musical chairs, but run around with your dogs. When you sit down in a chair you must also get your pooch on your lap—no matter what size she is!

Hide 'n' Seek: Scatter treats around the yard and let the dogs sniff them out.

Best in Show: On the invitation, ask guests to dress up their dogs. Then have a runway showdown and give out silly awards like "Best Dressed," "Most Likely to Date Tinkerbell Hilton," or "Fuzziest Friend."

DRINK!

salty dog sodas

BOW-WOW YOUR FRIENDS WITH THIS REFRESHING MOCKTAIL.

For each mocktail, wet the rim of a glass. Pour some salt into a small plate. Dip the rim of the glass into the salt to coat the top. Add 2 teaspoons of sugar and 1/4 cup of pink grapefruit juice and stir. Fill the glass 1/4 of the way with crushed ice. Pour ginger ale over the ice—be careful it will fizz up so pour slowly. Stir well. Garnish with a candied grapefruit (or other citrus fruit) ring. Repeat for the rest of the drinks.

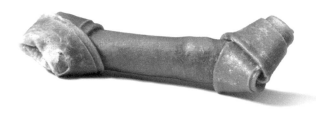

EAT!

doggie day menu

Entrée: Hot diggity dogs with assorted toppings: Ask an adult to help you grill hot dogs. Then set up a hot dog bar with a variety of toppings—use some standards (ketchup, mustard, pickles) and also some weirder options (salsa, sour cream, or baked beans!). Challenge guests to create the craziest dog and give a prize to the *weiner*! Ha!

Side: Poodle noodle salad: Get a few containers of macaroni salad at the supermarket. Serve it in a big colorful bowl and call it by this fun name—it's all about presentation!

Dessert: Devil Dog Icebox Cake

Drink: Salty Dog Sodas

Dog Treat: K-9 Layer Cake

EAT!
devil dog icebox cake

INGREDIENTS

- 1 pint cherry vanilla ice cream
- 10 creme-filled devil dogs or other creme-filled devil's food cakes
- 1 1/2 cups heavy cream
- 1/4 cup confectioners' sugar
- 1/2 teaspoon vanilla extract
- chocolate syrup
- 5 or 6 maraschino cherries

MAKES 8 SERVINGS.

1. Leave the ice cream on the counter for up to 30 minutes to soften.

2. Line the bottom of a 9 1/2x4x3-inch loaf pan with wax paper. Place 5 Devil Dogs width-wise in the bottom of the pan. Spread softened ice cream in an even layer over the cakes. Place the remaining 5 cakes width-wise on top of the ice cream layer. Cover with plastic wrap and place in freezer until the ice cream is very firm, at least 3 hours or up to 1 day.

3. Beat the cream, confectioners' sugar, and vanilla in a medium bowl with an electric mixer on high until it holds stiff peaks, about 3 minutes.

4. Remove the pan from the freezer. Run a sharp knife around the inside edges of the pan to loosen the cake.

Place a serving platter over the pan and flip over. Gently tap to release the cake. Peel the wax paper from the cake. Smooth whipped cream over the top and sides of the cake with a spatula. Lightly cover with plastic wrap and return the platter to the freezer to let the whipped cream firm up, at least 3 hours or up to 1 day.

5. Remove the cake from the freezer. Drizzle chocolate syrup over the cake to give it some decorative flair and garnish with the cherries. Slice the cake and serve!

doggie don't:
Chocolate is very harmful to dogs so don't share this treat with your pets!

EAT!
k-9 layer cake

THIS MEATY TREAT WILL TURN YOUR
DOGGY GUESTS INTO PARTY ANIMALS!

INGREDIENTS
- 1 bag dry kibble
- 1 can wet dog food
- 2 cups shredded cooked chicken
- 6 strips of cooked bacon

MAKES ABOUT 12-16 DOG SERVINGS.

1. Fill the bottom of a 9x12-inch cake pan with about an inch of dry kibble. Using a spatula, spread an even layer of wet dog food over the kibble. Place another layer of kibble on top, followed by another layer of wet food.

2. Sprinkle the shredded chicken on top and then lay the bacon strips in a row across the cake.

3. Scoop out and serve small pieces on paper plates to each pup.

CG! tip: Make sure to label the food so guests don't confuse people food with puppy food!

party pup-arazzi!

Turn a friend or sibling into the party pup-arazzi. Ask them to take Polaroids (or digital pics to send later) of each guest with his or her dog. At the end of the party hand out the photos as souvenirs.

dog-friendly downloads

- "Who Let the Dogs Out," Baha Men
- "Puppy Love," Lil Bow Wow
- "Animal Instinct," the Cranberries
- "Hound Dog," Elvis Presley
- "Wild Thing," the Troggs

come-as-you-are
halloween party

Forget those tired old Halloween parties. Throw this come-as-you-are costume challenge and your friends will think you're wicked cool! *Boo*-yah! $

hilarious halloween invites

Color-copy funny grade-school photos of you and your friends in costumes during past Halloweens. Glue them onto orange cardstock and write or print out the party details underneath the photos. Hand them out and get ready to make your friends howl…. with laughter!

> **CG! tip:** Don't worry too much about going overboard with the decorations. The goal of this party is to get your costumes together and get out quick so you can get in quality trick or treat time. You can always come back to your house at the end of the night to swap sweets—and to return any items borrowed from one another.

spectacular spooky setting

■ Play campy horror movies on mute as background décor.

■ Download spooky sounds (chains rattling, creaking doors, howling ghosts) and funny music (check out our iPod list for suggestions) to play while you're getting dressed.

■ Blow up some of the photos you used for the invitation on a color copier and hang them around the room.

■ Freeze plastic spiders, mini rubber eyeballs, or gummy worms in ice trays and use the cubes in everyone's drink for a creepy surprise!

■ Scare the pants off your guests (hey, they're getting changed anyway!) and place a few ghoulish items in unexpected places—like a rubber hand at the bottom of a popcorn bowl or a fake snake sticking out from under the coffee table.

60-minute costume challenge

Once everyone arrives, gather the troops for the pre–trick or treat activity—a race to create the best costume.

Ask each guest to come as they are (no costumes!) but tell them to bring at least one interesting piece of clothing (i.e., a plaid miniskirt, overalls, varsity jacket, leopard print leggings) and three or four other random items that could be part of a costume (i.e. bunny ears, plastic bangles, cowboy hat, crochet gloves). For your part, gather some clothes plus as many items around the house that could potentially become part of a costume (see "DIY: Costume Corner" to get you started). Don't forget scissors, markers, tape, construction paper, safety pins, and any other arts and craft supplies that could help put the costumes together. When everyone arrives, place all the items in the center of the room, set the timer, and go to it. You can work together or compete to create the best, most creative outfit.

diy: costume corner

See if any of these random items spark a spook-tacular idea!

- kitchen apron
- stuffed animal
- sunglasses
- shower cap
- old clothes from your dad, like ties, fedoras, sports jackets, and suspenders (ask him first!)
- large garbage bags
- toilet paper
- beach towel
- paper coffee filters
- duct tape
- leaves (scoop some off the front lawn)

CG! inspiration
LEFTOVERS—SPAGHETTI AND TOMATO SAUCE

Need help getting started? Look what you can do with only aluminum foil and saran wrap!

For her: Put on a strapless bra and short shorts or a strapless bikini. Take large sheets of aluminum foil and wrap them around your body. Tape them to your clothes so they'll stay in place. Cut out a large piece of paper or cardboard and label yourself so it looks like a piece of masking tape.

For him: Wrap a bright red towel around his midsection and run clear plastic wrap over it five or six times to create texture. Tape the edges down so they stay put. Slip on red shoes or sneakers and chunky red socks. Make a matching label and attach it to him. (P.S.: This doesn't have to be a couple costume, you can go as leftovers with a girl friend too!)

EAT!
devil's food surprise cupcakes

SERVE THESE TRICKY TREATS WHILE YOU WORK ON YOUR COSTUMES.

INGREDIENTS

- 4 cups all-purpose flour
- 1 1/2 cups unsweetened cocoa powder
- 2 1/2 teaspoons baking soda
- 1/2 teaspoon baking powder
- 1 teaspoon salt
- 1 1/3 cups (2 2/3 sticks) unsalted butter, softened
- 3 1/3 cups granulated sugar
- 6 large eggs
- 1 tablespoon vanilla extract
- 3 cups whole milk
- M&Ms
- candy corn
- 1 tube red and 1 tube yellow food coloring
- 1 (16-ounce) tub vanilla frosting

MAKES ABOUT 24 CUPCAKES.

1. Preheat the oven to 350°F. Line 2 12-cup muffin tins with cupcake liners.

2. Combine the flour, cocoa powder, baking soda, baking powder, and salt in a sifter and sift into a medium bowl. Set aside.

3. In a large bowl, beat the butter, sugar, eggs, and vanilla with an electric mixer on medium speed until fluffy. Reduce the speed to low. Alternate beating in the flour mixture and the milk, a little at a time, until well blended.

4. Fill each liner two-thirds of the way with batter. Bake 25 to 30 minutes. To see if they're ready, stick a toothpick in. If it comes out close to clean, they're ready! If it has batter on it, return to the oven and check every 3 minutes until they're done.

5. Let the cupcakes cool for 30 minutes. With a knife, carefully cut out a small square on top of each cupcake. Scoop out a quarter-sized amount of cake with a spoon and put several M&Ms or candy corns into the hole. Replace the square piece to cover up the hole.

6. Add 12 drops of each food coloring to the frosting. Stir until the frosting turns bright orange. Frost, then decorate the cupcakes with candy— how boo-tiful!

TAKE AWAY!
pumpkin autographs

Hand out mini-pumpkins and permanent markers, then ask all your guests to autograph each other's for personalized souvenirs.

scary soundtrack

- "Thriller," Michael Jackson
- "Monster Mash," Bobby "Boris" Pickett
- "The Time Warp," Rocky Horror Show Original Cast
- "Ghostbusters," Ray Parker, Jr.
- "Theme from Jaws," John Williams

> **! CG! party lines**
>
> ❝I love to throw Halloween parties. I decorate the house with fun spider webs and ghosts so it looks like a haunted house. If you pull cotton balls they will become stringy and look like webs. I also get a piece of cardboard and cut out a foot-print shape, then I take glow-in-the-dark spray paint and make foot-prints from the end of my sidewalk all the way to my front door. For the final scary touch I take red spray-paint and splatter it on the sidewalk around the foot-prints. My friends love coming to my parties and we watch scary movies and laugh about how those things totally wouldn't happen in real life."
>
> —Hailey, Greenwood Lake, NY

notes

CHAPTER 4
the impromptu
party

the impromptu **party**

Red carpets and caviar are extravagant and chic, but even a veteran party girl needs a break from all the formality. Sometimes she wants to slip into comfy jeans, let her hair down, kick back, and chillax with her closest pals. A get-together doesn't

have to be crazy, over-the-top to be successful. In fact, the best memories are often made at impromptu gatherings that take no planning or effort at all. Read on for tons of laid-back ideas, and when you're done chilling out, check out the bonus section on celebrity parties for inspiration so you can get back to the fabulous life of…you!

thank god it's **friday...**

Or Monday, or Thursday, or any day really! Here is a week's worth of excuses to get happy and gather together.

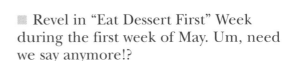

- It's your half birthday. Why wait another six months? You deserve a second party, now!

- Celebrate "Talk Like a Pirate" Day on September 19 (talklikeapirate.com). Argh, Matey! Invite your friends over to walk the plank and watch Johnny Depp!

- You finally got your hands on a Wii. Virtual tennis, anyone?

- Declare a Backwards Day. Turn those clothes around and boogie on down!

- Throw a "Recycle Your Prom Dress" party. You know you want an excuse to wear it again.

- Revel in "Eat Dessert First" Week during the first week of May. Um, need we say anymore!?

- It's the anniversary of the day you met your BFF. Don't remember? Make up an official date together and celebrate!

party planning express

No fuss, no muss. Here are eight stress-free shindigs you can plan with one day's (or even less!) notice.

Toga party: It's easy, cheap, and fun! All you need is a bed sheet, a cute belt, and a crown of leaves. Perfect for watching the Olympics or your favorite fraternity flick—and also for practicing your fabric wrapping skills. Break out the pita bread, order in some tasty gyros, and go Greek tonight!

Game night: Turn off the laptop, give TiVo a break, and bond with your friends the old-fashioned way: over a night of board games. Go old school with classics like Monopoly, Operation, Pictionary, and Life or challenge your friends to newer interactive games like Scene It?, Cranium POP 5, or Trivial Pursuit Pop Culture DVD. Stock up at areyougame.com.

Movie after-party: Take a cue from Hollywood. After any big movie premiere there's always a fun party. Keep the good times rolling after you leave the theater and invite everyone back to your place to gossip about the film and compare notes. Hit the concession stand once more before you head back to snag some midnight snacks.

Pizza party: A no-brainer, for sure. Say cheese—or pepperoni or mushroom—and we bet your friends will be over faster than the Domino's guy! Everybody's favorite food is worthy of a solo celebration, but if just a pizza party is too plain for you, serve it up at any of these other casual affairs (Pizza and Painting? The perfect combo!)

pizza perfecto

Did you know that 29 percent of you prefer to eat pizza at a party? Chocolate came in a close second, followed by chips and salsa. Mmm…salty and sweet!

Study buddy night: Two heads are better than one. And three, four or five heads are even better still—and enough for a low-key study session. For every chapter you cover take a break for some brain food (i.e., snacks!) and serious socializing—now that's a brilliant idea, Ms. Smarty Pants!

Painting party: Are you redecorating your room? Get by with a little help from your friends and turn your renovation into a celebration. Lure guests over with yummy snacks and the promise to repay the favor anytime they need it. Then pop on some overalls, crank up the tunes, and get to it.

Around the world party: Explore new foods and all your friends' houses by ordering different kinds of takeout.

Start at your place with your favorite ethnic cuisine. Serve a few tasty appetizers, mingle for a while, and then move on to the next venue for a different food experience. Aim for four or five (preferably nearby) houses. Don't feel like shuffling around? Have everyone bring their dishes to one location and turn it into a foreign food bazaar!

Fall TV season: The wait is finally over and your favorite characters are coming back. Record all of your favorite shows for the week, then have everyone over for a lazy Saturday season premiere marathon. Veg out for the day, order in your favorite takeout and screen them all at once.

For tasty recipes to serve at any casual shindig check out "Casual Friday," page 58.

party in a box

The opportunity to celebrate could be right around the corner and a true party girl would hate to miss out—so she's always prepared. Take a few of these items, add good friends, stir things up and *voilà*, instant party! Keep some of these goodies around the house—or in your locker, purse, or car—for a party-on-the-go.

- glow sticks.
- confetti.
- mini bottles of bubbles.
- tiara: Everything is more fun when you're wearing a sparkly crown!
- Hello My Name is…nametags: Great for icebreakers—instead of names have guests write in a funny adjective that describes them (Hello My Name is…Flirty and Fabulous!), or stick the nametags on paper plates as impromptu place settings.
- the perfect party mix CD.
- breath mints.
- colored bulbs: Change out the brights for more soothing mood lighting.
- disposable camera: Don't miss a single memory.
- fancy drink umbrellas: Even tap water feels festive with an umbrella in your glass!
- yummy scented room spray: Transport your guests to a tropical island, a coffee house or an autumn hayride with just a few spritzes!
- twister!: Left foot red, right hand yellow—what better way to get to know your crush?

TGIF!

party like a **star**

No one knows how to get down better than the rich and fabulous. But you don't need a million bucks or a famous parent to throw a supersonic soiree. You just need to know a few insider secrets. And we've got them. So practice your picture face…with these celeb inspired tips and tricks you can host a mega-watt party that might just make front page news!

the seven celebration commandments

Most celebrity bashes live by these rules. Follow their lead and we bet your next party will have the paparazzi in a flash-frenzy!

Wow them with the invite. The invite sets the tone and psyches guests up for the party to come, so be creative. Mariah Carey sent personalized video messages to her guests' cell phones for her Grammy party. See, it doesn't cost a lot to make a memorable invite—it just takes imagination. Now, let yours go wild.

Push your theme to the max. When celebs throw a theme party they go all out to create a big buzz—like Diddy's famous annual White Party in the Hamptons, where guests have to dress in head-to-toe white (undies too!) to

get in. Just pick a theme—all pink, 70s, safari, whatever! Then be sure to follow it all the way through. For your party, think of every possible place you can add theme details and your event will be over-the-top.

Always keep them guessing. A celeb-worthy party has to have an element of surprise to wow guests. At one celebrity fashion show and charity event, Kanye West gave an unexpected performance. Usher had live panthers at his VMA after-party. And when Volkswagen launched a new Jetta, they had acrobats hanging from the ceiling at their party. So maybe you can't fly in J. Lo for the night, but you can do something unexpected or edgy. Invite a friend who's moved away (don't tell anyone—let them be surprised when she shows up!), or bring out your friend's band to play a surprise set.

Give guests the star treatment. Paparazzi, velvet ropes, a guest list, and VIP rooms make celebs feel like they're the chosen ones. It's easy to create this feeling of exclusivity at your bash— have a burly guy friend play bouncer, make a VIP list for him to check, roll out red fabric, and have another friend snap photos of guests as they arrive. You can even rope off a VIP section of the room or put "Reserved" cards on some tables.

Don't forget the DJ. The hot trend is for celebs to DJ big parties—Lindsay Lohan likes to take charge of the DJ booth at her parties. To keep everyone pumped, ask your friend with the most-wanted iPod list to guest DJ your event. Set up a fold-out table as a DJ area and make up forms so everyone can submit requests—you'll keep the party going all night!

It's not over 'til it's over. Don't let the end of the party fizzle out. Make the last impression that everyone has of your event as amazing as the first part and do something fabulous—like bringing out root beer floats at midnight or revealing that there's a treasure hunt to find hidden party favors. It's that easy to guarantee your party will be "front page" news the next day at school.

the impromptu **party**

Did you know...
that 55 percent of CosmoGIRL!s say that a party's not really a party unless you're serving ice cream cake? Bring on the sporks, baby!

Send them home wanting more. The celeb way to end a fantastic party is with a fantastic bag of swag. Stars leave events with tons of loot and celeb gift bags can include thousands of dollars worth of cool stuff. But you can give guests something just as memorable without dropping loads of cash. DIY personalized shirts with cheap tanks from Target and rhinestones or search online for cheap theme-related gifts, like mini disco balls for a 70s party.

steal these sweet ideas

Celebrity party planners know the presentation of the cake can make or break a party. Try their expert tips—delish!

- Keep your cake or dessert covered until ten minutes before you cut it. That way it will be a surprise when you unveil it (*voilà!*) and nothing can ruin it beforehand.
- Can't afford an elaborate cake? Fake it! Decorate stacked boxes so they look like they're covered in frosting. Then fill them with yummy cupcakes.
- Forget a cherry on top! Try white chocolate covered strawberries.
- Make the cake part of the fun by letting your guests create their own. Start with a basic yellow cake and put out bowls of icing, fruit, chocolates, and candies so they can choose their own toppings.
- Choose extra-long sparkler candles to add extra flash. Plus you'll have more time to blow them out—and that means more time to come up with one ove-the-top birthday wish!

memorable movie moments

We picked our favorite, most inspirational party scenes. Rent these films to prep for your next blowout. And the CG! goes to...

Best Entrance

Rent: *A Cinderella Story*

Fast forward to: Sam coming down the stairs at the school costume party.

You'll learn: How to arrive fashionably late, look gorgeous, and snag your Prince Charming!

Best Impromtu Party

Rent: *The Breakfast Club*

Fast forward to: The gang dancing on the library railing.

You'll learn: A good party is all about who you're with...not where you are (even if it's detention)!

Best Hostessing

Rent: *Breakfast at Tiffany's*

Fast forward to: Holly Golightly's house party.

You'll learn: How to rock an LBD (little black dress!) and make throwing a party look effortless and chic, Dah-ling!

Best Sleepover

Rent: *13 Going on 30*

Fast forward to: The slumber party in Jena's apartment.

You'll learn: No matter how old you get, best friends, 80s music, and playing dress-up is the best way to boost your mood.

Best Birthday

Rent: *Sixteen Candles*

Fast forward to: The end! A birthday cake, a dining room table, and Jake Ryan. Yum!

You'll learn: Sometimes a party of two is all you need!

Best Dinner Party

Rent: *Beetle Juice*

Fast forward to: The dinner party, of course!

You'll learn: Dinner parties can be stuffy but calypso music and a séance will shake things up!

Best Graduation Party

Rent: *Can't Hardly Wait*

Fast forward to: What fast forward? The whole thing is one big party scene!

You'll learn: To appreciate your friends and the moments you have together.

Best Party Hook Up

Rent: *Romeo + Juliet*

Fast forward to: Leo and Claire locking eyes through the fish tank.

You'll learn: Be flirty and coy and let him come to you!

Best Exit

Rent: *She's All That*

Fast forward to: Preston's party where Laney goes with Zack.

You'll learn: How to keep your cool, no matter what happens. And never let them see you cry—wait 'til you get outside!

honorable mentions:

FIVE MORE MOMENTS IN MOVIE PARTY HISTORY

Risky Business: Watch Tom dance around in his skivvies. Then think twice before you throw a party behind your parents' back!

Animal House: Way before *Old School*, there was this original college party flick. Watch it before rushing a sorority.

The Wedding Crashers: Check your guest list. You never know who might be crashing your party.

Never Been Kissed: Drew was right—when in doubt turn it into a costume party and you can't go wrong!

Beach Blanket Bingo: Check out this squeaky clean classic. Then add a little 50s retro flair to your next beach or pool party and it'll be far out!

😮 CG! ouch: **birthday suit!**

❝ For my birthday party a couple years ago I had a whole bunch of my close friends over and we were watching TV. My mom called me upstairs to help her with something. I was upstairs for about 10 minutes when I started to hear a bunch of laughter coming from all my friends. I went downstairs to see what happened, and it turns out my dad was showing them videos of me from when I was young—and I was naked in most of them! It was the most embarrassing thing ever and lots of people at school found out. My friends still remind me about it. My dad thought it would just be fun to show them cause I was soo cute...yeah right!"

notes

CHAPTER 5
the after **party**

the after **party**

All good things must come to an end, CosmoGIRL! And we know that after the hard work, the preparation, and the anticipation leading up to your party, the morning after can sometimes hit hard. The trick is to take your mind off it by focusing on all the after party activities you have to take care of—like straightening up, sending thank yous, and organizing your pictures. Oh, and our favorite way to get over the after-party pouts? Start planning your next event! Because remember this: One successful party deserves another….and another…and another!

the big **clean up**

It's a dirty job but somebody's got to do it! And if you want your parents to green light your next gathering (see "Rated PG" page 126), you'll want to do it right. But it doesn't have to be a drag. We've got a three-pronged plan for making messes, well, less messy!

before

Clear out. Set up the party area to prevent accidents before they happen—move out (or cover up) any furniture or items that you don't want broken or spilled on.

Cover up. Use fabric to cover tables. At the end of the night you can just shake all the crumbs off outside, then roll up and send the cover off to the laundry room—your tables stay nice and clean underneath! If they're long and drape down, you can even protect the floors too.

Forget about fancy china. Make things easy with disposable tableware. Go green and choose an eco-friendly brand like Preserve (recycline.com). You can pop these sturdy recycled plastic plates, tumblers, and utensils right into the dishwasher and reuse them. Or scrape them off and recycle them when you're done.

during

Clean as you go. Clean up a little throughout the night so it's not a total disaster at the end. Try not to obsess over it or you'll miss all the fun, but if you're heading into the kitchen why not grab a few plates as you go? Or bring a paper towel to wipe up a spill in the hall on your way back.

Nip it in the bud. Keep an eye out for big messes like food globs that could leave a stain. Catch them early on and you won't have to spend hours scrubbing them the next day.

Make it easy for guests to "pitch" in. Leave a trash bag or can discreetly in a corner of the party room. If it's there, guests will be more likely to dispose of their trash when they're done. If you want to make a bigger deal of it, do it with humor—label the can with a big sign that says "Feed Me!" or another funny message so guests will get your drift!

after

Enlist a few willing guests. As the party winds down, see if your closest friends wouldn't mind sticking around a little longer to help. When you work together it will go faster and won't feel like a chore—plus you can rehash the night while you tidy up.

Clean to the beat. Everything is more exciting when you add music. So flip on some upbeat tunes that will keep you motivated and shake your booty as you straighten up.

Work logically. Start in the party room and bring all the food, drinks, serving bowls, and plates to the kitchen. Next, make a run through the house (check the hallway, bathroom, and any other rooms that might have been used) and collect any stray items. Then once everything is completely cleared, tackle the kitchen last.

Too pooped? If it's super late and you're too tired, make sure to clear away all perishable items and refrigerate leftovers. Leave the rest for the morning, then blow out any candles and get some sleep so you're fresh for AM clean-up duty!

giving **thanks**

Merci, danke, arigato, grazie. It doesn't matter how you say it, a thank you is always welcome. Check out these thank you do's and don'ts.

DO send a handwritten thank you note if you received a gift.

DO personalize the note for each person. Mention the specific item and say something nice about it or how you might use it.

DO try to send a note as soon as you possibly can—no later than a week after your party.

DO keep a batch of cute notecards on hand. You never know when you might need them. Check out the huge variety of thank you notes at cafepress.com, where you can even create your own customized cards.

DON'T forget who gave you what. Keep an organized list of gifts and givers and check each one off when you've sent a note. (Use our handy list at right.)

DON'T feel obligated to send handwritten notes for a party where you didn't receive gifts. But a casual short e-mail or even an e-card thanking everyone for coming to your event is a nice gesture and is always appreciated.

DON'T underestimate the power of the thank you note! It seems like a pain, but people like to be appreciated and they may be more likely to do something nice for you again. Score! (Not that you should write notes just to get more gifts, sister!)

rated **pg**

You may be the star of the night, but you can't forget those folks behind the scenes, a.k.a. your parents. Of course you want to feel like you're running the show, but it is their house—so you need to respect your mom and dad's needs too. If you do you'll discover that respect is a two-way street—the more you can do to show them that you'll be a responsible hostess, the more likely they are to leave you alone (well, for the most part!) and stay quietly out of the picture. Keep them updated on your plans, ask for their opinions and advice, and approach your party in a mature way by creating a budget, working to earn some cash, calmly negotiating, and compromising when you butt heads on certain issues. And, of course, thank them for all their help.

thank-you **list**

gift	from	thank you note: ✓
		☐
		☐
		☐
		☐
		☐
		☐
		☐
		☐
		☐
		☐
		☐
		☐
		☐
		☐
		☐
		☐

get **over it!**

Got the post-bash blues? We've got the cure. Here are seven ways to cheer yourself up when the party's over.

1. Make a creative breakfast with left-overs. Think candy corn omelets and corn chip–coated hash browns. Or when in doubt, a slice of cold pizza always does the trick—yum!

2. Meet your best friends for a gossipy "party-roundup" brunch.

3. Download your party pics and fill in our scrapbook pages so you won't forget a thing.

4. Update your online profile and blog all about the juicy tidbits of the evening. Hey, you may become the next Perez Hilton!

5. Hit the bathroom mirror and practice new makeup looks to debut at your next event.

6. Don't forget to snap pics and put them in your party flipbook so you can duplicate them later (see page 35).

7. Now that you've been bit by the hostessing bug, start planning your next big bash—flip through magazines to get inspired for themes and décor, rip out some pages, and start a party inspiration file.

CG! ouch: guilty party!

"I was getting ready for a party at my grandma's house. It was cold out, and the only sweater I could find was my brother's new white one, so I took it. At the party my friend accidentally spilled her red drink on it. I went to the bathroom to clean it—the room reeked of you-know-what, but I had to clean the sweater. After I was done, someone knocked on the door, and it still smelled. I didn't want them to think it was me, so I sprayed perfume; that only made it worse! Finally I just walked out. Well, the guy who was waiting goes, 'Oh my god, did you just take a dump?' I was so embarrassed!"

photo finish

Try one of these creative ways to display all your party pics. They'll look great in a snap!

Magnetic attraction: Turn pics into magnets that you can stick in your locker or on the fridge. Buy magnet paper at an art supply store. This special paper has a sticky side—you peel the paper off and place the photo neatly on top. Then cut the photos into different shapes or cut around your bodies to create silhouettes. Cute!

Stick 'em up: Print your photos on printer sticker paper. Then stick on your notebooks, your folders, or your bulletin board. If you've got a lot of pics, turn them into a whole sticker book at moo.com.

Great wall: Blow your favorite pics up on a color copier (or get a copy shop to do it if you want to go super big) and paper an entire wall of your bedroom with them. Use double-sided tape or Fun Tack so you don't ruin the paint. Then invite your friends over to see your life-size party pictorial!

Block party: Purchase a wooden cube at a craft store (they come in varying sizes). Trim photos to fit each side of the cube, then use rubber cement to attach them neatly. Smooth them down so there are no wrinkles or lines. Make two or three blocks and stack them on your desk. Then flip them around to change up the photos on view.

Drinks on you: Turn party pics into coasters to use for your next party. They'll be a huge hit! Check out the Oscar party on page 72 for info on how to make them.

CLICK CLICK!

the after **party**

my **party**

Don't forget to copy this page so you can fill it out for all your parties!

Date _____

Here's who came _____

_____

_____

_____

_____

_____

_____

My theme was _____

_____

My invite was _____

_____

_____

My décor was _____

_____

_____

I wore _____

_____

_____

_____

I served _____
_____
_____
_____

The icebreaker was _____
_____
_____
_____

We played _____
_____
_____
_____

My party soundtrack included _____
_____
_____
_____

My favors were _____
_____
_____
_____

My favorite party moment was _____
_____
_____

paste your favorite **party pictures here**

paste your favorite **party pictures here**

resources

Your go-to guide for all of your party throwing necessities.

invitations

notecards, cardstock, invitations, etc.

Kate's Paperie: katespaperie.com

Kinkos: fedexkinkos.com, 800-254-6567. Great for making color copies or shrinking and enlarging photos.

Paper Style: paperstyle.com

Papyrus: papyrusonline.com

Pearl: pearlpaint.com. The ultimate art supply store. You'll find cardstock, paper, and all the supplies you need when you're DIYing your invites.

Robin Maguire: robinmaguire.com

Staples: staples.com, 800-3-STAPLE

electronic invites

Evite: evite.com. Digital invites plus great extras like a budget calculator, checklists, and a personalized notebook for storing all your party planning notes.

punxsutawneyphil.com for electronic e-vites

other goodies

Café Press: cafepress.com

California Paper Goods: papergoods.com: for blank jigsaw puzzles

Container Store: containerstore.com; for takeout cartons

Skimaps.com: for ski slope maps

décor, favors, and games

general decorations and favors

Oriental Trading: orientaltrading.com

Party America: partyamericastore.com

Party City: partycity.com

Partypop.com: Find vendors in your area for everything from balloons to DJs to makeup artists and more.

Party Fair: partyfair.com

Pearl River: pearlriver.com, 1-800-878-2446

Pier 1 Imports: pier1.com. Cute serving pieces, faux flowers, throw pillows, and tons of candles!

Plum Party: plumparty.com

theme supplies

Aloha Home Décor: surferbedding.com

Halloween Adventure: halloweenadventure.com, 1-877-U-Boo-Too

Hollywoodmegastore.com

Party Supplies Hut: partysupplieshut.com

Party Theme Shop: partythemeshop.com

Pinatas.com: 888-746-2827 ext. 24

other goodies

Allposters.com: for posters

Areyougame.com: for games

Blaircandy.com: for plastic footballs

Campmor.com: for hand warmers

Demeter Fragrance Library: demeterfragrance.com; for scented room spray

Dylan's Candy Bar: dylanscandybar.com; for lunchboxes

Oriental Trading: orientaltrading.com; for novelty items

Paper Snowflakes for Children: papersnowflakes.com; for snowflake instructions

Standard Concession Supply: standardconcessionsupply.com; for popcorn boxes

Tabletopics.com: for conversation starters

craft and fabric stores

A.C. Moore: acmoore.com

Jo-Ann Fabric and Craft Stores: joann.com

Michael's: michaels.com, 800-MICHAELS

paper goods, cleaning supplies, and miscellaneous housewares

Bed, Bath and Beyond: bedbathandbeyond.com, 800-GO-BEYOND

Kmart: kmart.com, 866-KMART-4U

Moo.com: sticker book maker

Preserve: recycline.com; for recycled plates

Target: target.com, 800-440-0680

The Container Store: containerstore.com, 888-CONTAIN. Boxes, envelopes, and bins to hold favors, display snacks, or to organize your party supplies.

Wal-mart: walmart.com

food and drink

BJ's Wholesale Club: bjswholesale.com

Candy4u.com: for candy

Candywarehouse.com: Stock up on cheap, bulk candy—including fun novelty items like sushi-shaped candy.

Cocktailcandy.com: for rim glasses

Costco: costco.com

Dylan's Candy Bar: dylanscandybar.com, 888-DYLANS-NY

Krispykreme.com: for donuts

Krittersinthemailbox.com/product/cookiecutter.htm: for cookie cutters

Popcornfactory.com: for popcorn

Serendipity3.com: for hot chocolate mix

Trader Joe's: traderjoes.com. Yummy unique snacks and lots of organic options.

Your local supermarket: Don't forget your basic supermarket can be a cheap and easy way to stock up on everything from a custom cake to shrimp cocktail—talk to the different counters (bakery, deli, etc) about what you need.

photo credits

index

food and drink index